This is one of those rare "how to" books where the author truly delivers the goods. He gives down-to-earth information and advice on where to look for a job that's right for one's skills, how to land that job and—perhaps most important—how a job seeker looks to the recruiter on the other side. Everyone needs that "something extra" to land a great job. Because of a more competitive market place and the ongoing restructuring of many businesses, looking for a job today is arguably more difficult than at any other time in recent memory. In the same way business executives try to strategically position their companies to take advantage of changing economic circumstances, so too must job seekers strategically position their job searches to get the most advantage from their competitive strengths. Mangum's *99 Minutes to Your Ideal Job* is especially timely. I recommend reading it as the first step in any job search. In fact, read it before you begin your resume.

Norman R. Augustine, Chairman and Chief Executive Officer
Martin Marietta Corporation

Bill Mangum has written a job book that's brimming over with practical ideas. His research of thousands of corporations and job seekers clearly identifies what employers want and what job seekers must possess. The techniques for finding a job are dramatically different from even five years ago. Mangum explains why the rules have changed and what rules you must follow today to be successful. Don't permit your career to be filled with misunderstanding, missed opportunities and unintended conclusions. Begin to take responsibility for your career with *99 Minutes to Your Ideal Job*.

John W. Poynton, President
Clark, Poynton & Associates
and President, *Association of Outplacment*
Consulting Firms International

Finally, a no-nonsense guide to braving today's topsy-turvy job market from one who knows it inside out. Bill Mangum cuts through this thicket with a steady hand, a clear head and years of executive search experience. Read this before you try to sell an idea—or yourself. In our economy, you can't afford not to.

Nancy K. Austin, Co-Author
A Passion for Excellence

Any job hunter would be well advised to read Mangum's new book. It's extremely sound advice from a well experienced and knowledgeable executive recruiter. It's practical and basic enough to be of interest to a new entry to the job market as well as for the experienced job seeker. Mangum has written in a very concise, real world style, what's effective and valuable to any job hunter in today's jobs market.

Don Butler, President and CEO
The Employers Group (The oldest/largest employers organization in the USA, dealing exclusively in human resources management)

EMPLOYERS REJOICE!
We will be seeing many more quality candidates who are properly prepared in their job search. Mangum's new book will undoubtedly make job hunters and employers both winners. This book is solid homework for the serious job hunter. So many job hunters that we see today are poorly prepared, but I predict that every job hunter who follows the 99 Minute Formula will improve their effectiveness 90%! Mangum has been a successful search consultant for over 30 years for Northrop Grumman and I believe he's covered all the bases in his new book.

David Suydam, Corporate Vice President, Human Resources Development and Planning
Northrop Grumman Corporation

Today, each of us must clearly define how we are going to move ahead in our chosen field while faced with the possibility of being displaced several times during our career. Mangum's book provides the answers to the many "how do I" questions when a job search is undertaken and includes the key "99 Minute" formula for presenting ourselves to prospective employers. The "road map" he provides is clear and to the point, providing insights and guidance garnered from his extensive experience and the surveys he conducted. I have worked with Mangum for years as a client and as a job hunter/search placement. From my personal experience, his suggestions are right on target.

Lloyd Gomez, Plant Manager
Robertshaw Controls Company

99 Minutes to Your Ideal Job is state-of-the-art information and advice about how to crack the new job market, from someone who knows. It's a small amount of time well spent toward saving precious time and trouble in your job search.

David A. Lord, Editor
Executive Recruiter News/Kennedy Publications

This is a book that every professional should read, whether or not they are currently involved in a job search. Mangum placed me in my present position. *99 Minutes to Your Ideal Job* makes available to the world the advice that was previously only available to candidates like me with whom he has worked. Mangum understands these times and what it really takes to land "that job, the ideal job." This book will help you in much the same way that Bill helped me and many others like me.

Barry Altman, President and CEO
SWIFT-COR

99 Minutes to Your Ideal Job should be a required read for all job hunters. All too often, today's job hunter is abused by unfounded gimmickry, misdirected by entrenched myths and biases based on yesteryear's job market, and confused by vague or ambiguous "answers" to their job search questions. I found *99 Minutes to Your Ideal Job,* on the other hand, to be engaging, well organized, focused, actionable and—most important—based on substantial, current fact. The book imparts an accurate picture of today's job market; the 99 Minute Formula really breaks down the steps of a job search into understandable, doable activities, while it weaves useful and relevant employment and hiring manager and job hunter suggestions with perspectives garnered from extensive survey work.

Michael R. Forrest, Executive Director and CEO
College Placement Council, Inc.

No organization or individual in today's job market can ignore the ever-changing nature of the work environment and thus the changing job market. Change is the norm! To grow and prosper in today's challenging dynamic environment, individuals need to carefully assess themselves and the organizations with which they are seeking employment. Individuals need to build a foundation of competitive, up-to-date skills, flexibility and demonstrated customer/client focus. These are attributes that organizations like my company look for. *99 Minutes to Your Ideal Job* is an up-to-date and forward-looking job guide for those seeking to becoming successful job hunters in today's competitive, ever changing business world and job market.

Warren I. Mitchell, President
Southern California Gas Company

99 Minutes to Your Ideal Job is time well spent learning to negotiate in a world no longer defined by job security, but by career stability. Mangum's book helps men and women who are seeking new jobs as well as human resource professionals with constantly changing personnel needs. In plain English, Mangum shows how you can put your best foot forward in a job market with little patience for past laurels.

Michael R. Losey, CEO and President
Society for Human Resources Management

This upbeat guide is for every job seeker. Recent grad, grizzled veteran; white collar or blue. It will fire up your drive, fuel you with the right stuff, and guarantee you the pole position in the most vexing race in America today. . . finding the *right* new job in an era when every employer's middle name is "Grinch."

John R. Sibbald
John Sibbald Associates, Inc., Executive Search Consultants;
author, *The Career Makers, America's Top 100 Executive Recruiters.*

Very comprehensive; covers all relative points with regard to job search; good factual support.

Randolph W. Westerfield, Dean
School of Business Administration, University of Southern California

A solidly professional, practical guide for individuals seeking employment as well as for individuals who are seeking to fill positions in their companies in these times of change. Mangum has written a most timely and authoritative book on the basics of finding and obtaining satisfying employment. This book is a must read for any job-seeker who seriously seeks the job he/she wants. It is a step-by-step guide that will ensure how to be ready and equipped to handle any job opportunity quickly. The review of past historical trends, survey results and suggestions at the end of each chapter are true testaments of the value of the book. I have had the good fortune to utilize Mangum's skills in securing a senior level position and in addition have used his skills and directions successfully on many occasions as a client, including outplacement. He is exceedingly perceptive on what is happening in corporate America and the job market. I cannot emphasize enough to job seekers the importance of following the formula presented in this book.

Gilbert C. Apodaca, Corporate Director of Human Resources and Administration
Alcoa Composites, Inc. Aluminum Company of America (ALCOA)

99 Minutes to Your Ideal Job is an important insight to the job market for those making career transitions. Based on solid survey information from every component of the market, it is a practical guide to job hunting for everyone beginning that process. From the savvy perspective of search professionals, the insights from hiring managers, and the view from previous job hunters, this book is a unique collection of views of the job market.

I highly recommend the book as a practical working guide for everyone entering the job market.

Jim Stiggett, Senior Vice President, Human Resources
DFS Group Limited;
President, IACPR—*International Association of Corporate and Professional Recruiters, Inc.*

99 Minutes
to Your Ideal Job

William T. Mangum

John Wiley & Sons, Inc.
New York • Chichester • Brisbane • Toronto • Singapore

This text is printed on acid-free paper.

Library of Congress Cataloging-in-Publication Data:
Mangum, William T.
    99 minutes to your ideal job / William T. Mangum.
        p.   cm.
    Includes index.
    ISBN 0–471–11125–2 (cloth) — 0–471–11126–0 (paper).

Printed in the United States of America

10 9 8 7 6 5 4 3 2 1

This book is dedicated to all who are seeking a better, more satisfying, and rewarding job—the ideal job.

Every individual is involved in a personal journey. Your job and your career lead to success or serve as a detour. Taking charge of your job search, finding the ideal job, and avoiding detours is what this book is all about.

About the Author

William Mangum is president of the Thomas Mangum Company, an executive search company founded in 1964. The Company has served a broad spectrum of companies including major *Fortune* 500 corporations, medium- and small-size companies in a variety of businesses and industries. As its long-term president, Mangum has been selected by a number of his peers as one of the leading executive search consultants in the industry. He is listed in the *Career Makers; America's Top 100 Executive Recruiters*. Previously, his company was selected number one in a survey conducted by the Southern California Technical Placement committee. Over the last decade, in a continuing effort to gather data on the changing job market and its impact on both job hunters and employers, Mangum has published numerous job market surveys for his business.

Mangum's background involves extensive experience in executive search at all levels of the organization structure, workforce planning, organization planning, and organization development. His background also includes line and staff management experience in human resources management, operations, and P & L management. In addition to executive search assignments, he has assisted in major research and state-of-the-art build-up programs. Such searches have included finding advanced technology, scientific, engineering and management talent for breakthroughs in a variety of industries and technologies. Among them have been searches for the leading aircraft/aerospace and missile/space executives, and teams for roles in advance exploration, such as the Apollo program (moon landing), Viking Mars program, and Stealth program.

Contents

Acknowledgments

A heap of thanks and praise to the many people who helped shape this book—1200+ survey respondents, thousands of job seekers, hundreds of potential executive search candidates, and hundreds of employers. I am grateful to all of you for sharing your experiences and job journeys. To the hiring managers, human resource directors, and candidates, thank you for an enlightening journey. To the individuals who conducted the surveys, a particular thanks is due for your devotion and interest in gaining knowledge about the ever-changing and dynamic job market medium within which we work. Thanks, also, to Carolyn Carter, a most able associate of some 11 years, who labored through manuscript preparation and typing. Melinda Stephens sifted through thousands of words, editing and offering advice. I am indeed indebted to her. To my wife, Maria Elena, a thanks for patience and understanding. I greatly appreciate everyone's contributions.

Introduction

In recent years I have received thousands of telephone calls and over 50,000 resumes from job hunters in most areas of industry and business throughout the country. Many of these individuals have asked for help in finding a job, and most have asked for an overview of the job market as it relates to their individual job search needs, qualifications, and skills. In the last several years a surprising number of job hunters have needed a reorientation into the realities of today's job market due to the dramatic changes that have occurred.

99 Minutes To Your Ideal Job is my response to the tremendous ongoing request for answers to job hunter's questions about finding a job and handling the job change/search process. Executives, managers, professionals, white-, and blue-collar workers of all levels are seeking help and guidance in larger numbers than ever before due to today's lean job market.

As an executive search company president and consultant, I have created a new view and time perspective (99 minutes) on winning the ideal job. This view is substantiated by recently completed (1993–94) multiple national job market surveys of three thousand employed and unemployed job hunting executives, managers, professionals, and hiring managers; and from two employer surveys (1993–94) of the employment market involving four thousand employers.

During the last ten years or so, employers have found that they must increase both quality and productivity dramatically in order to compete in both domestic and global markets. To meet these demands, employers are seeking employees with skills and experience that are an exact match for the requirements they must fill. Therefore, a more knowledgeable job search effort is required for job hunters to satisfy an employer's needs and be successful in their job search.

> To find the ideal job today, job hunters must know today's job market, and they must be able to respond to the changing needs and upgraded demands of employers.

My conclusions are based on today's lean job market conditions described in Chapter 1, the world changes affecting the job market cited in Chapter 2, and the numerous surveys conducted, including the recent surveys reviewed in Chapter 3.

Unlike the booming job market of the past, today's job market is an *employer's market* where job hunters face stiff competition and must be prepared to give their best effort in order to attain the ideal job. To be really effective, this effort must focus on the key 99 minutes encompassing the job hunter's presentation to an employer. The 99 minute time frame provides a guide for the job hunter that includes developing/gaining employer interest, successful interviewing, and getting results/offers. I use the term *99 minutes* to pinpoint the pivotal time frame a job hunter must deal with because ultimately all job search efforts focus and funnel through this time frame. The nucleus of this 99 minute time period is the time frame job hunters have to present themselves and their skills to a potential employer. Therefore, these 99 minutes are the most important minutes in a job hunter's search.

In the following pages, you will learn how to apply the 99 minute formula in today's dramatically changing job market and the job search process. You will learn to use it for analyzing your skills capability, job sourcing, developing a job search plan, marketing and selling yourself, gaining an employer introduction, successfully presenting yourself, and polishing your image. You will also learn the meaning of the new guides recommended here and the following acronyms and their importance in job hunting: WOW candidates, VWP, PEG matching, TNT, and TART. Most important of all, for the highly competitive mid-1990 to 21st century job market, you will gain an understanding of the need to match very closely your skills and experience to employment market needs and specific employer needs.

99 Minutes To Your Ideal Job begins with three vital preparatory chapters on the job market, followed by the *99 Minute Formula* and winning job search approaches and techniques. The first two chapters will give you a jump-start into understanding today's job market and the vast changes that are occurring. Chapter 3 includes the national job market survey results. Chapter 5 gets you organized to take charge of your job search. Other Chapters give you the hidden key to job search success, clues to how employers recruit and select new hires, and the new job search guides.

Job seekers will find excellent information and some startling figures here in regard to

- Salary and job levels being offered in today's job market
- Employer attitudes toward hiring
- The most effective job sources
- Job search sources and techniques that are working
- Employer contacts required to obtain an interview/offer
- Consulting and temporary work
- The recareering dilemma
- The impact of the *ten year economic cycle*
- What the new lean management style means
- Hiring activity projections

All the vital up-to-date information, methods, and techniques you need to know about your search are here. At the end of every chapter you will find a list of suggestions from hiring managers and successful job hunters on how to better prepare for today's challenging and competitive job market. A careful study of the information provided can make a difference in time spent wisely in your job search, and most importantly in finding the ideal job. A job search workbook is available separately. (See last page of book for more information on this.) This workbook provides additional exhibits, working samples, checklists, and a detailed breakdown of a job search plan and the job search process.

1

Job Hunting for Success
In Today's Job Market

Job seekers today must have job-hunting survival skills to be successful in the competitive job market of the mid-1990s–2000 era. They must be willing to go beyond the traditional job search methods of the past. They must face frank truths about dealing with employers in a lean business world—a job market that is radically different from yesterday's, where new approaches are necessary.

Fact 1: In 1994 the U.S. government reported economic growth of 4.7 percent for the third quarter of 1993, the greatest economic growth in five years. In the same month this report was released, U.S. companies announced planned layoffs of some 108,000 employees. These layoffs are believed to be the largest ever recorded in a one-month period for such a widespread spectrum of U.S. industry.[1] This in the face of resounding economic/business news.

If you want to obtain a better position in today's changing job market, you must adapt to this new business era. To do so, you need an up-to-date education. You need to know:

- The economy's impact on business activity and the job market
- The changing world's impact on your job search
- New strategies for business and hiring

---

1. "Productivity Index Rises Moderately," and "Major Firms' Planned Layoffs Sets Record," *Los Angeles Times*, 9 February 1994.

- The best ways to develop job opportunities and approach a prospective employer
- The *99 Minute Formula*

As you embark on your journey for a new job, you will likely find it will try your patience and challenge your skills. There is no question that today's job market is different and, for many, difficult. A positive attitude can make this rigorous task both stimulating and enlightening—in fact, a real adventure!

Fact 2: In the past five years, a record 1.4 million executives, managers, and administrative professionals lost their jobs. In the five-year period between 1981 and 1986, only 782,000 lost their jobs.[2]

Easy-to-find jobs are a bygone element of the 1970s and 1980s. The generally robust employment market of past years is over, and may not return for years to come. Job hunters today must adjust to the realities of a tougher job market as companies become locked in global competition with smaller and higher quality staff and organizations.

The new factors in the business and economic equation are created by changes in global/domestic competition compounded by more controlled, regulated, litigated, and financially constrained business management. These factors require companies to have a more productive, flexible, and profitable workforce. As a result, a new operating mode has evolved in American commerce known as *Lean Operations Management.* In other words, a new business era has emerged.

Companies have been forced to refocus on the basic tasks of running a business and why, where, when, and how they utilize their workers. These dramatic and historical changes are affecting millions of people, resulting in far fewer jobs, often at different and more difficult skill levels.

As you begin your job search, you will discover you are facing a very different job market than in past years. You may also find there are some new skills you need to learn in order to meet an employer's needs for the competitive marketing requirements of the mid-1990s and beyond. Your goal should be to make sure you are aware of all the requirements needed for the job area in which you are competing.

After doing your best to match these requirements, you will be

---

2. Ibid.

way ahead of the game by following the job search process described in the following chapters. To be an aware job hunter, you must know what capabilities an employer requires in today's job market. This is an education in itself. And that is what this book is all about.

> The vital information you will discover here comes from 30 years of experience managing executive searches. This experience involves conducting job searches for hundreds of employers involving thousands of job hunters in the executive, professional, and management job market.

Whether you are entering the job market for the first time, thinking about a job change, or have already left your job—either voluntarily or involuntarily—the survey information included here will allow you to utilize feedback from thousands of job hunters, employers, and hiring managers.

The survey questions cover a wide gamut of the ups and downs a job hunter encounters in today's job market. You will find the following list of questions, many of which were asked in the survey, representative of ones you might ask. Answers are provided to each question in appropriate chapters throughout the book.

1. How long does it take to find a new job?
2. What are the more effective ways to find a job in today's job market?
3. What are the best ways to develop job opportunities and approach prospective employers?
4. What specific job sources should be used and which are most effective?
5. Approximately how many employer contacts are required to obtain an interview and an offer?
6. What type and length resume should be used?
7. How effective are unsolicited resumes mailed to employers?
8. What percentage of unsolicited resumes result in interviews?
9. What are the conditions of the job market?
10. What trends are appearing in the job market in regard to hiring?
11. What jobs are reported in demand and available?
12. Should I quit my current job before looking for another position?
13. What percentage of employers offer outplacement assistance for terminated employees?

14. My approach for a new job, including my resume, is not working. What suggestions do you have?

Your most important question of course is: How successful will my job search be? The *Job Hunter Surveys* (see Chapter 3) indicate that many job hunters have to substantially revise their search methods to successfully compete in today's job market.[3] This is due to fewer jobs, lack of employer interest, and minimal interview opportunities.

According to the surveys, it takes an average of 6.24 months to find a new job in today's market. When a new job is found, it often pays an equal or smaller amount and offers equal or less challenge than the previous one (survey Chapter Three). This, of course, is what you want to avoid if at all possible.

Survey results show a job market reacting to dramatic change. For approximately a decade, American business has been shifting gears to deal with debt burdens and the need for greater efficiency in extracting more and greater profits in increasingly competitive markets.

New challenges in the business world, such as those created by growing global markets and nations that assist their companies in research, have created intense competition, both nationally and internationally. This places pressure on American companies as never before. The past ten years of restructuring, mergers and buyouts, downsizing, layoffs, workplace reengineering, and workforce redesign have resulted in the greatest changes in American business since the Industrial Revolution (see Chapter 2). The result is an extensively downsized workforce and a larger number of unemployed all attempting to adapt to a changing and more complex evolving business world.

The evolving business world encompasses a much more competitive national and global economy. This economy adds several new factors: A North American Free Trade Pact, a more open Russian business climate, a growing South American market, and the emergence of a united Europe. Combine these factors with increasing competition from other powerful areas like Japan, China, and Southeast Asian countries, and you have pieces of a puzzle that fit very differently than those of previous economic eras.

In order to stay competitive, American companies are responding to this evolving business world by operating lean—and to some people mean. They are laying off; selling divisions and business units;

---

3. In Chapters 2 and 4 you will see how to approach the job market today vs. what worked successfully in previous years, particularly in the booming '80s.

and downsizing (what we now call *right sizing*). All this in an attempt to adjust to economic realities.

> These historical changes are affecting millions of people. Not only are there fewer jobs, those who fill them are expected, in many cases, to perform at more advanced skill levels and to display a more sophisticated degree of knowledge than in past years.

In subsequent chapters, you will see how you can adapt to these changes. As an executive, manager, professional, blue-, or white-collar worker, you have in recent years been part of a repetitive story — the ongoing revitalization of American business and industry through restructuring, reorganization, downsizing, rightsizing, layoffs, and terminations.

Now you can become a knowledgeable and successful job hunter. The surveys of hiring managers and employers throughout the country will give you a clearer picture of the job market and what employers are looking for as they fill positions key to their companies' future growth. Following are a representative selection of questions asked.

1. In what career fields and positions do you experience the greatest difficulty in recruiting qualified candidates?
2. In what career fields do you see the greatest applicant surplus?
3. Are employers screening candidates differently today, that is, are they looking for a higher degree of skills than previously required?
4. Are specific qualifications or skills required of job applicants in today's market that were not required in the '80s?
5. Are employers screening applicants more carefully today to adapt to changing business conditions?
6. What types of resumes are preferred? What features have the greatest positive impact? Which make a negative impression?
7. What is the length of time taken to review a resume?
8. What percentage of unsolicited resumes will likely result in interviews?
9. What type of candidate shortcomings are observed most often in today's market?
10. What's happening in the job market now . . . what's it like out there for job hunters?
11. What is the level of activity completed by job hunters in their search efforts and what is the effectiveness of such activity?

As you proceed with your job search, keep in mind the overall big picture. This picture shows that to be a successful job hunter today you have to be the person who receives the job offer—often out of hundreds and sometimes thousands of candidates who apply. This is a very different scenario from the past years of a booming job market. What has worked for many job hunters in the past 20 years will no longer open magic doors of opportunity in the mid-1990s. For many years companies competitively searched for talent in a job hunter's market. A total reversal has occurred today. We are now in an employers' market. To be the person chosen today, you must find a way to stand out over your competition and preferably above the employer's objectives. This book is dedicated to pointing you in the direction of becoming the outstanding candidate for the position you seek.

> The first impression you make and your initial presentation count above all others. They are the reason the *99 Minute Formula* is so important. This is where you are either separated from the masses or buried with them.

Therefore, the letter you write and the resume you enclose must uniquely qualify you for the position you seek. Your background, skills, experience, and personality must stand out. Also important are your approach to and knowledge of the job market (research and sourcing), your use of the job search process, plus the preparation and execution of your job search plan. Your marketing and presentation effort (the *99 Minute Formula*) becomes the key foundation for a successful job search.

To give you some idea of the number of people I have been involved with in job search assignments, consider the following: Each search assignment is most often developed from a large list of prospects to a potential candidate population ranging from 20 to 100 individuals per position or assignment. This has allowed me the opportunity to work with many outstanding people—close to 50,000 total, with about 5,000 turning into prospective candidates, and some 1,500 into serious candidates.

This experience gives me insight into the job market from both sides of the fence. It gives me the ability to match employer needs with potential candidates' interests and requirements to the benefit of both parties. I wrote this book to help you put all of the ingredients together for an effective, well-targeted job search effort. I believe this will lead you to the ideal job, which you can effectively win or easily lose in just 99 minutes.

Talks with business leaders, hiring employers, executives, and job hunters from all over the country contribute to a picture of a job market teetering between slow growth and fewer jobs. The anxieties of both job hunters and employers are projected in the process of getting to know each other as future daily working partners.

One of the most frequent questions I am asked is how to change jobs more easily and effectively for a more ideal job. In the present employment climate, this question is particularly crucial for those faced with a job change and the financial crisis period that may accompany a layoff or termination.

> Our national surveys indicate that many successful job search methods previously used must now be modified, completely revised, or dropped and replaced with methods that are compatible with the world's current business era.

What has evolved in the mid-1990s is a business world very different from the one many people were accustomed to dealing with in the past. The surveys provide meaningful and solid data for planning and preparing your search, resume presentation, approach to the job market and the time frame you can expect to complete your search.

In these surveys the key aspects of the job search process become evident. You must:

1. **Know how to package your capabilities and experience and how to present yourself.** The presentation of your skills, and talents to match current employer needs is critical. The *99 Minute Formula* and the four new working guides will help you get the job done and get the job.
2. **Know yourself.** Be aware of your talents, skills, and interests, particularly your special talents and skills. Look for a company culture compatible to you. It helps to choose a position and employer that blends with your interests and lifestyle. Utilize discipline and ingenuity to put yourself ahead of the pack.
3. **Know the job search process.** Know what steps are required for an effective job-search effort. It is important to understand the whole process in order to find the position you seek.
4. **Know the job market.** Be aware of what jobs are available and when. Know where the jobs are and how to obtain them. Know how to work the behind-the-scenes and hidden job

market and how to develop potential jobs. Study the economy in order to compare growth areas to your background, skills, and interests.

5. **Research your sources.** Good homework is a necessity. Good research and sourcing can ultimately be the behind-the-scenes key to a successful job search effort. Between the sources you develop and who you know and what they know, your sources will multiply in what can become an endless chain. The challenge will be to narrow your choices down to a viable framework.

6. **Develop a plan.** Decide who you will contact for a job prospect and how. What method of presentation will you use? Decide when and if you will send out resumes, how you will follow up, and what you will wear to your interview.

7. **Execute your search.** Don't just sit there thinking about your search. Complete your resume in a format, style, and length that works for today (see Chapters 3 and 10). Organize your sources and resources and execute your plan of action. Develop a job search plan, go to the mailbox, pick up the phone, develop a routine, and stick to it. Most important, match your talents and experience to an employer's needs. A mismatched effort is a waste of your time!

8. **Market yourself.** Be creative in displaying your talents. Position yourself ahead of the pack. Make your background and experience unique to the position for which you are applying. Know your strengths and don't be bashful about selling them (see Chapters 5–12 for winning job-search techniques, gaining employer interest, and interviewing).

9. **Follow up and know how to close the interview.** It's essential! In addition, you must know how to evaluate, negotiate, improve, and close an offer.

10. **Start your new job off on the right foot.**

You can view the current job market in terms of restrictions. However, you would be much wiser to view it as a challenge, an opportunity, and an adventure—a study of the business world as it relates to your career interests. The more you know about what's going on in the business world, the more you will be exposed to job opportunities—and the more you can contribute to bright innovative conversation in a job interview.

Why did Armand Hammer open a pencil factory in Russia over 70 years ago? Because everyone in Russia needed to write with something, and pencils were more economical than pens. Why did Mc-Donald's journey to Russia in recent years? Because Russian food is coarse and bland, and the soft spicy taste of a McDonald's hamburger is like a bite of heaven to the average Russian. McDonald's is eating up the profits!

Why did Mrs. Fields market her uniquely rich and delicious chocolate chip cookies? Because it stands to reason that if Mrs. Sees' chocolate candy appeals to the masses, so then should Mrs. Fields' mouthwatering cookies. And they do. Mrs. Fields has had to restructure her company to compete in this lean and mean business climate, but she's succeeding, and she's already done very well in her job quest! Interestingly, neither Mrs. Fields nor Mrs. Sees went to college, but that didn't stop them. If there is a credential you don't have, be creative and find a substitute. Or earn that credential in the real world of experience as Mrs. Fields and Mrs. Sees have done.

You can view competition with fear of failure or you can view it with the excitement of knowing you can give your all to being the best you can be. The best dressed. The best informed. The most organized. The most skilled. The most dependable. The competitor with the most is prepared to deal with today's job world.

> Today's business world finds itself in the midst of major changes, many of which dramatically impact the job market, the company employment function, the workforce, the labor market and a company's ability to effectively deal with its workforce and labor market.

In the following pages, you'll discover how to market and sell yourself—how to polish your image. You'll be clued into the employer's selection process and learn how to delineate myths from truths on finding the job that suits you best.

Job source information is key to your search. You'll find a wealth of source material here, material that exists because of a new era in communications sparked by a very competitive world economy. From this information, you will be able to tailor your job search to you and the job market.

Despite big changes in the job market that have resulted in fewer jobs, you can turn such adversity into opportunity. By being exposed to ideas that will broaden your job search horizons you can develop and create opportunities.

Your attitude will be the most important asset you possess in obtaining the job you seek. As you embark on your journey, be sure to have some fun along the way! Yes, there will be ups and downs. For some there will be difficulties, frustrations, and rejections. Remember, however, that adversity breeds the motivation for success. Adversity forces you to fight for your ambitions. It forces you to learn, thereby giving you new ideas and insights. Many accomplishments can come from new discoveries made in the job search learning process. Much enjoyment will come from the new places you visit, the people you meet, and the new friends you make. When all is said and done, the excitement of your new job offer will no doubt make up for the difficult job search you have completed.

The business world is waiting for you to join the competition!

SURVEY SUGGESTIONS

From Hiring Managers

- Be computer literate.
- Be persistent.
- Have realistic expectations.

From Job Hunters

- Be prepared for surprises and disappointments.
- If let go, negotiate outplacement with current employer.
- Be flexible.

2

The Changing World's Impact on Your Job Search

If you have been job hunting, you most likely have been affected substantially by the changed business world and economy of the '90s. The changes are so extensive they are greater than most individuals in the past experienced in an entire career.

The business world is predicted to remain in a lean mode for years to come.

> This means far fewer jobs are available, and a restructured U.S. business world is seeking broader skills and greater talent from job hunters in order to be profitable in a competitive economy.

Business and economic cycles tend to have a life of their own. They run their course by responding to market and economic conditions. The current business and economic cycle is still evolving with its own life force, as past cycles have done (see Exhibit C, Ten-Year Cycles, on page 23). As a result, it is doubtful one can expect a major change in this cycle and, therefore, in management's attitude, consumer response, and the job market, anytime soon.

> The downsized, restructured company of today, operating in a reengineered lean and mean format, is working successfully. To the surprise of many, it will continue to be an operational style for many years to come.

Some companies—IBM, Boeing, and Sears, for example—have only recently implemented this operations style with substantially leaner work forces.

11

Companies have changed in ways that many people in the job market have just begun to realize. In the '70s through the early '80s, companies often prided themselves on the number of people they hired and, in many cases, the number of vice presidents, business groups, size of corporate staff, and layers of management and staff they had available. Today, the reverse is the case: We're in a new lean business operating cycle for the tough new mid-1990s–2000 era.

> As a result, American business is making an ongoing effort to be more competitive, improve quality and productivity, reduce costs, minimize staff size, reduce debt burden, and thereby improve efficiency in an environment emerging from a generally deflationary economic setting.

Companies are looking for a lower break-even point and more flexibility. Hence, they are in no mood to staff up as in past years. Companies today are not, in general, investing in chancy projects to build up and/or support staff. The marketplace still has many companies wanting to improve and gain a competitive edge. Some companies are still struggling to survive. Some are casualties of acquisitions, mergers, and buyouts. Many companies have closed their doors. Others are doing better than in the recession years of 1991 and 1992 with good operating results, yet are still either not hiring or only adding a small number of new hires (see survey results in Chapter 3).

There are so many forces at work in today's business environment that it is difficult to fully comprehend the changes taking place. In a meeting for which one of the concerns was the job market, President Clinton stated:

> The world is changing so fast that we must make aggressive, targeted attempts to create the high-wage jobs of the future. That's what all our competitors are doing.[1]

The Changing Business World

A brief review of the various forces involved will give you a sense of what has created the changing business world in which we now live.

---

1. "Jobs: Workforce Changing in America," *Los Angeles Times*, 7 April 1993.

(The items marked with an asterisk are explained more fully in Chapter 3.)

Forces Driving Business World Change

- Global competition*
- Intense domestic competition*
    (driven by quality and productivity improvement)
- Debt burdens
- Banking/Savings and Loan credit crunch
    1988 Basel Agreement on bank's capital standards
    Savings and loan debacle
- Concern about health care benefits and regulations
- Government-supported foreign competition
- Recession of '90–'92
- Sputtering/slow-moving economy*
- Intransigent government
- Increasing burden of government regulations on employers
- Fundamental change in corporate management*
- New management philosophy* (lean operating management)
- Technology advancements
    Information processing and telecommunications
    Automation
    Computer chip evolution
    Personal computer utilization
    Entertainment and education technology evolution
- Government bureaucracy
- Reengineering the workplace
- Cost of government compliance
- Legal system entanglements
    Worker's compensation
    Sex discrimination
    Frivolous litigation
    Environmental regulations
    Consumer liabilities
- And more . . .

These forces and others are putting pressure on business and industry to keep costs down, resulting in an almost paranoiac atmosphere of cost reduction/control and workforce management. A major factor in keeping costs down is workforce costs. Employers must decide whether to maintain or reduce the workforce levels and weigh the pros and cons of hiring permanent staff for expansion.

Major attitude shifts are occurring in regard to hiring, compensation, benefits, workforce levels, use of temporary help, contract workforce, and less costly plant and facility locations, among other things. A reengineered workplace is evolving with a downsized and restructured workforce as its standard operational format. Flatter organizational structures are becoming the norm, with far fewer levels of management and a substantial trend toward participative management and self-directed workforces. This all adds up to fewer job openings. Companies are slow to hire and in many cases hire only out of necessity. Companies today are painfully selective in hiring and, in almost all cases, are only interested in upgrading the overall skill level of the organization.

How Companies Avoid Adding New Hires

In many cases, companies are exploring other ways to handle full time replacement needs and new hires. These include:

- Temporary help and short term help
- Dividing workloads
- Extensive computer utilization
- Information technology application
- Increased automation
- Overtime
- Increased training of existing staff
- Job sharing and job stuffing
- Reengineering the workplace and tasks
- Increased cross-functional training and activity
- Self-directed workforce and participative management methods

This bottom-line thinking has been utilized by companies who have been forced to refocus on the basic task of running a business more profitably, often in a more debt-burdened environment, and are now faced with growing world competition. A growing world market, in a diminishing regional recessionary climate involving increased global competition, offers one of the biggest challenges yet faced by American employers.

During a meeting in which one of the concerns was the job market and America's competitive position in the market, President Clinton stated, "Economic growth depends as never before on opening up new markets overseas and expanding the volume of world trade."[2]

The education and training that some job hunters possessed in the past will, in many instances, no longer be sufficient in the current competitive job market. Job content, hours, and locations are changing. Demands on worker contributions are increasing as workforce demographics change. Putting in 35–40 hour weeks is not enough to survive and progress in today's business world. In coming years, substantial additional job training, on and off the job, will be required for those who want to get ahead in the new competitive business world.

It usually takes a substantial period of time for business cycles to change and for management operational styles to catch up to the current cycle. If, for example, companies had begun downsizing earlier in the '80s, the recession of the early '90s may not have been felt so dramatically by job hunters. We are now in the downsize phase of what most consider a major management shift from overstaffed organization to lean and mean understaffed organization. Management may not realize it may have gone too far in its reductions, restructuring, and other downward changes until the mid-1990s have come and gone. It likely will continue its lean management trek into the late 1990s.

Job Market Changes

For today's job hunter the changes that are occurring are both good news and bad news. While these changes have brought about job reductions in certain areas, opportunities have become available in new and related fields of the future as a result of these changes. Some analysts estimate the rate of job generation during the next ten years will barely match the growth of the labor supply. Assuming this evaluation is partially true, today's job hunter must assertively pursue all opportunities. These opportunities include jobs not openly available on the surface of the job market. These jobs can be developed by assertive job seekers in the behind-the-scenes and hidden job market. For example, thousands of job opportunities are being developed by those seeking new careers as entrepreneurs, consultants, service advisors, and franchisers.[3]

---

2. "President Clinton's Inaugural Address," *Los Angeles Times*, 20 January 1993.
3. Shown by the *Job Hunter Surveys* and discussions with job hunters.

A bright light on the horizon for job hunters is the growth projected by the U.S. Department of Labor, Bureau of Labor Statistics for technical jobs and professional/white-collar support jobs. It also projects growth in many service industries.

Forecasts by the Department of Labor predict a 26 percent expansion in professional and technical jobs between 1988 and the year 2000. By the turn of the century, this is projected to become the largest single occupational category of workers. Twenty-three million jobs and a major change in the demographics of the workforce population are projected.[4] Secretary of Labor Robert Reich states:

> To guarantee a strong recovery we must create half a million jobs. . . . jobs that rebuild our highways and airports, jobs to renovate housing, to bring new life to rural communities, and spread hope and opportunity among our nation's youth. . . . Our plan looks beyond today's business cycle, because our aspirations extend into the next century.[5]

A recent Bureau of Labor Statistics prediction indicates that job growth will be fastest in higher skill, higher pay occupations (managers, professionals, technicians, and executives), which comprise approximately a quarter of today's workers. The Bureau of Labor Statistics predicts 41 percent of all job growth until the year 2005 will occur in these areas. The mid-1990s–2000 period may well be the time in which professional and technical employees move from the periphery to the core of the U.S. labor workforce.

Exhibit A (see pages 17–18) shows the employer/job market changes that have occurred in recent years. It provides a comparison between the business world that existed from 1960 to 1990 and today's business world.

The Job Market and the World

A look at the changes that have occurred in the U.S. and world economic and geopolitical environment, as shown in Exhibit B (see pages 18–20) will help you understand more fully the forces you must deal with in the job market of the new business era.

---

4. "A Changing Economy," *EQW Issues*, Sept. 1992.
5. "Labor Secretary Robert B. Reich is Turning his Low Profile Post into Powerhouse," *Los Angeles Times*, 7 June 1993.

Exhibit A: Employer/Job Market Changes

Today	1960–1990
Recession recovery—Essentially a jobless to limited-job recovery	Substantial job recovery from prior recessions
In the last five years 1.4 million executives, managers, and administrative professionals have lost jobs as reported by Bureau of Labor Statistics	During the five-year period 1981–86, only 782,000 jobs were lost
No jobs or minimal jobs available	Many jobs available—often lack of talent
Extensive job competition	Minimal job competition
Rightsizing/downsizing	Liberal hiring (Some companies begin downsizing prior to 1990.)
Restructuring	Companies add new managers, vice presidents, groups, and departments.
Limited pay increases	8–12 percent standard increases
Performance pay rather than regular yearly increases	Regular yearly increases and merit increases
Substantial temporary help and short-term employment	Unrestrained hiring
Reduced fringe benefits	Progressive substantial benefits; some cafeteria-style benefits
New job offers with less compensation and lower increases	New job pay increases (8–20 percent range)
Minimal relocation allowances other than standard moving expenses	Extensive assistance, up-front bonus-home sale
Fewer/limited management opportunities; fewer promotions	Extensive internal growth, many VP positions, directors, managers, etc.
Longer work hours, more overtime, more job responsibilities	Extensive new hiring and use of consultants
Present job now includes work previously done by several people (job stuffing)	Minimal multilevel assignments and little overloading of work
Employee/employer joint health care	All employer-paid care
Lean operating mode; minimal hiring of replacements or no hiring	Considerable hiring of new staff and most replacements

(continued)

Exhibit A *(continued)*

Today	1960–1990
More constrained employee expense accounts; minimal car allowance and fewer autos provided	Employer-provided auto and expenses; less-constrained expense accounts
In many cases marginal company growth/no growth and reduced sales in others	10–25 percent market growth
Flat organization structures	Many middle-level management and VP positions
Midmanagement positions eliminated along with substantial staff and executive positions	Many junior executives and considerable hiring of MBAs for management positions

Exhibit B: U.S. and World Events or Situations Impacting the Job Market

Events or Situations	Results of Events or Situations
End of cold war, collapse of Soviet empire	Major reduction in defense spending and loss of millions of jobs; extensive downsizing of defense industry, restructuring, mergers and acquisitions
Substantial reduction of U.S. military forces	Return of thousands of ex-military to job market
Transnational economy	Short-term drain on U.S. companies
Fundamental changes in management philosophy— lean operations management	No hiring or limited hiring
Reengineered workplace/staff	Reduced staff needs
Global domestic competition	Drive to reduce costs and thus lower wages
Quality/productivity trend	Improve customer satisfaction, products, and services; substantial training and retraining of U.S. workforce
1980s freewheeling boom economy; merger-mania, overhiring; buyouts of mid to late '80s	Extensive downsizing, reduction, layoffs, early retirement plans, etc.

(continued)

Exhibit B *(continued)*

Events or Situations	Results of Events or Situations
Increased debt burden in many U.S. companies	Adjustments to new debt burden; downsizing, restructuring, sellouts, etc.
Downsizing/restructuring	Many layoffs, but improved profits and market conditions, reduced spending, and operational costs, less hiring
Operating lean and mean	Debt-burden reduced, competitive position enhanced, improved profits, lower break-even point, less hiring
Reduced government income	State, county, and city government funding constrained, potential layoffs
Reduced corporate profits for some companies domestically and in Europe	Reduced budgets procurement and hiring
Reduced educational expenditures	Reduction in many school districts, teacher salaries, and school expenditures
Recession 1990–1992	Cutbacks; layoffs of millions of employees due to reduced income, profits, and consumer spending; fundamental management philosophy change
Credit crunch, banking changes and restrictions; construction, real estate slowdown	Layoffs; hundreds of thousands of people impacted by industry slow down and change
World hot-spot dilemmas Iraqi War Emergency disaster relief Support of Russia Foreign aid commitment	Drain on economy; government resources not being spent on domestic and business/industry, welfare, and educational needs
Minimal U.S. trade barriers	Nonlevel playing field in some areas
U.S. debt burden	Enormous strain on economy
Technology advancements , e.g., microchip improvements, PC evolution, software development, information systems, computer controlled processes, medical/drug breakthroughs	New markets and products, new jobs in some areas; also job obsolescence and job loss

(continued)

Exhibit B *(continued)*

Events or Situations	**Results of Events or Situations**
Savings and loan debacle drain and resulting Resolution Trust Corp. bailout	Financial losses plus additional costs, time, and paperwork
Decline in manufacturing employment	Loss of over 150,000 manufacturing jobs in 1992. (Prior loss in second half of this century showed decline in blue-collar workers—from 48 percent to 28 percent—largely in manufacturing.)

Many of these changes, while positive, cause job loss or obsolescence and place many people in a transition mode. Changes that put business and people in transition include the following:

- Quality improvements
- Productivity improvements
- Examination of executive/management effectiveness
- Examination of workforce usage
- Reengineering of workplace
- Criteria changes in performance measurements
- Changes in salaries and compensation
- More rigorous performance standards for incentive programs
- More rigorous benefit and health care program evaluation
- Greater involvement by board of directors
- Pay scales tied to performance
- Core products emphasized
- Shedding of unrelated business/acquisitions
- Big business operations reviewed as to effectiveness
- Restructured business organization (i.e. flat organizations), downsizing/rightsizing, cutbacks, plant closings/consolidation

Many economists say and some business signs indicate the last years of the 20th century will be a tepid era involving a lukewarm economy, very different from the prior overall robust 40 years we were fortunate to enjoy. If this is the trend, you will see a new era of limitations, constrained business growth, companies continuing to manage in a tight operational mode, and an economy involved in slow overall growth.

The current economy has the potential for a number of cyclical ups and downs. The election of a Democratic President may offer some hope for some federal spending. There are predictions for federal government spending for public projects, for the infrastructure, and for job retraining. Special national needs, such as a national data-highway computer network, nonpolluting autos, upgrades in telecommunications, air traffic control, mass transit and rail technology, roads and related construction projects, health and welfare, are targeted. These, along with a general economic improvement, may move the economy out of its lackluster performance of the '90–'92 recession for a while and is sure to create some opportunities. It is doubtful, however, that federal spending will change the basic economic realities (lean management and less hiring) of the current decade, particularly during the mid-1990s time frame. The loss of 3 million middle-management jobs during the '80s is evidence of the transition that has taken place. The determining factors for job programs in the Clinton administration will be national debt considerations, budget constraints, the economy, and the existence of a Republican majority that maintains a watchdog vigil over public spending programs.

Unemployment remains a problem despite the end of the recession—in the range of 5.7 to 6.5 percent of the workforce. When combined with the number of people working part-time who can't find full-time employment, and discouraged workers who have dropped out of the market, the real total unemployment figure is higher than has followed prior recessions.[6]

The U.S. Department of Labor reports this last group has shown little improvement over the past several years and remains well above previous recession recovery levels. Thus, the recovery from the recession has been limited in terms of job growth, and is, in fact, the slowest recovery from a recession since World War II.

The potential for a prolonged job recovery with substantial hiring in the next several years is questionable, particularly when you combine all the factors of change previously discussed and consider the impact economic cycles have on recovery. In addition, the hard-

---

6. U.S. Department of Labor, Bureau of Labor Statistics, as reported monthly.

headed attitudes of many employers during the '90s may well delay a substantial job growth recovery, leaving many economists, writers, workforce watchers and Labor Department prognosticators guessing. The ongoing commentary in many leading publications—such as *Fortune, Business Week,* the *Wall Street Journal, Los Angeles Times,* and *New York Times*—provide many interesting insights regarding jobs and the job market.

Economic Cycles and Their Impact

Consider the lessons of past economic periods. They appear to run in prolonged ten-year cycles, as shown in Exhibit C (see page 23). Factor in what has happened in the last eight years to the world economy and geopolitical events (as described earlier in Exhibit B). You will probably conclude that the only elements appearing on the horizon to move the U.S. economy for *job recovery* are technological advancements and supplying exports and services to a larger portion of the world, along with some pump priming by the Democratic administration.

President Clinton, incidentally, provided some excellent advice for job hunters:

> We will find our new direction in the basic old values that brought us here over the last two centuries—a commitment to opportunity, to individual responsibility, to community, to work, to family, and to faith.[7]

A resurgent economy based on military spending will not occur as it has in the past, barring some unforeseen major confrontation or numerous limited confrontations. Moreover, an economy based on consumer spending, construction, and real estate growth will be slow in getting employers on a major hiring track in the mid-1990s.

Many firms are still smarting over the bulking up of staff during the '70s and '80s. During this time period they added layers of management and support, while coming off of a long-running robust economy, believing markets would grow indefinitely. Repercussions from the overstaffed '80s will take time to correct. A story familiar to many job hunters took place at one of America's Fortune 100 com-

---

7. "President Clinton's Inaugural Address," *Los Angeles Times,* 20 January 1993.

Exhibit C: Ten-Year Cycles[8]

1990s	Slow economic recovery, uneven and unpredictable. A reaction to growth in the '80s. Substantially reduced military/defense spending. Potential for continued limited growth and above average unemployment. Senior corporate management wants to be as lean as possible and assumes markets will be slowing.
1980s	Prolonged growth. This period contained the second largest expansion in U.S. economic history (92 months).
1970s	The inflationary '70s was often called the hangover decade, reacting to the stimulative policies of the '60s. Two wage freezes and four price control phases. Massive jump in energy prices. Early aerospace recession.
1960s	The soaring '60s, pushed by stimulative economic policies and progressive military spending, registers the longest expansion in history (106 months). The unemployment rate dropped to just over 3 percent.
1950s	Consolidation followed the '40s war and post-war growth era. Prices jumped and conservative economic policies cooled inflation, resulting in several recessions.
1940s	Substantial growth was created by the war years and the stimulus of high military spending outlays for conversion of industry for defense. Unemployment disappeared. Early restrictions on civilian spending led to pent up consumer demands and therefore to consumer expansion. Set the stage for consolidation in the '50s.
1930s	The Great Depression: Thousands of businesses failed and millions of workers lost their jobs.
1920s	The Roaring Twenties—Substantial but uneven economic growth. Migration of millions to city life with sweeping changes of attitude and lifestyle following a restrictive period due to World War I. Led to stock market crash of 1929.
1910–1919	Wartime restrictions affected business and consumers. Considerable military and industrial development.

panies. It involved a substantial post-recessionary change. If you haven't experienced the downsizing/restructuring syndrome of a company, you'll better understand the motivations involved by putting yourself in a real-life story and in the position of the group vice president involved.

8. "Learning from the Past as We Enter Another 10 Year Economic Cycle," *Los Angeles Times*, 12 July 1992. ('90s projections updated by author.)

You are in a lengthy business meeting with division managers and operations staff circled around your conference table. Your CEO has just finished reviewing the comments of the group president, prefaced by a look of concern . . . almost doom. As the CEO speaks, you look around the table. Vice presidents are intently listening to every word, staff are leaning forward on the edges of their seats, all are awaiting the words most hoped would not come, although they were inevitable.

Finally, the CEO says, "Sell off the profitable group, where the business is not mainstream to the company's core business—and in the meantime, downsize immediately to attract the best possible price."

The directive is clear, and the message concerns you. The CEO of this profitable Fortune 100 company of excellent reputation and strong market position has just advised the key managers involved that it will sell its profitable special products group of four divisions totaling some $150 million in sales.

As group executive you say to yourself, "This doesn't make sense." You are sitting there with a sound business, including projected new products offering 15 percent growth over the next five years. Your mind wanders as the meeting continues—some eight hundred employees, a number of them devoted and with years of service behind them. Many will be affected, and a sizable number will be let go in the coming months as the result of the squeeze you will have to apply to make the figures look better for the group sale.

In preparation, you have been through this exercise mentally several times before. Now the world of reality faces you squarely. Your immediate focus is on one division, a president, three vice presidents (operations, technology development, marketing), a human resources director, a product assurance manager and an administrative manager. They're the first to go. In the next two months, further downsizing will result in reductions of two hundred additional people—as a starter. For the first time you wonder if you should think of moving on—changing jobs and beginning the job hunt. Almost immediately you're brought back to reality when the CEO asks you for your time frame for group reductions and how you expect to reduce your expenses by 18 percent immediately.

You pull out your prepared plans, which include sweeping and penetrating reductions along with a major reorganization. You know you must immediately begin dealing with hundreds of talented people who will leave the company in the next few months. You also know that with the group being placed on the market, you may soon be in the job market yourself and need to begin preparing for a job search or pursuing other alternatives.

Scenarios such as this have taken place all over the country. You must be prepared to deal with the vast changes in today's business world and learn where opportunities exist as well as where to turn up opportunities.

SURVEY SUGGESTIONS

From Hiring Managers

- Know the market and keep current with it.
- Target your market.
- Network.

From Job Hunters

- Stay current in your field.
- Get serious from day one.
- Prior preparation for job hunting is a necessity.

3

Job Market Surveys: New Tips and Trends to Help Job Hunters

In this chapter, the national survey responses will help you gain vital information on how to be a winner in today's job market. They provide current firsthand data, advice, and insights on working today's job market from successful job hunters, hiring managers, and employers. This knowledge will help you analyze the job market, develop your job-search plan, and execute your search for the ideal job.

The Surveys

The nationwide *Job Hunter Surveys* were conducted by the Thomas Mangum Company in 1993 and 1994 and involved 3,000 executive, management, professional, and technical personnel in the nationwide job market, including over 500 hiring managers.[1] The Job Hunter Surveys involved a 27 percent response in 1994 from 1,000 job hunters and a 20 percent response in 1993 from 2,000 job hunters.

The *Employment Market Survey of Employers* was conducted by the Thomas Mangum Company and the Employment Managers Association as a joint project in 1993 and 1994.[2] The first employment mar-

---

1. Thomas Mangum Company, *Job Hunter's Questionnaire for Executive, Management, Professional, and Technical Personnel,* 1993, 1994; Thomas Mangum Company, *Job Hunter's Questionnaire for Hiring Managers,* 1994.
2. The Employment Management Association (EMA) and Thomas Mangum Company, (TMI). *Employment Market Survey: Employer Assessment of Current/Future Employment Market for Executive, Middle Management and Professional Staff,* joint project, 1993, 1994.

ket survey of employers included approximately 2,500 companies in 40 industries with a 14 percent response. The 1994 survey involved some 1,500 employers surveyed in the same marketplace with a 14 percent response. A total of 7,400 job hunters and employers took part in the multiple surveys. Survey respondents to the *Employer Survey* were principally human resource executives, managers, employment managers, and staffing specialists. Each survey involved extensive multiple questions and only portions of each survey are reported here for purposes of brevity. Some segments of each survey are reported separately or in more detail in the individual chapters applicable to the topic. For example Job Sources (Chapter 8), Resume Preparation (Chapter 10), and so on.

Survey Results

A summary of the *Job Hunter Survey* data is presented first, followed by hiring managers' responses. Partial segments of the *Employer Survey* data follow, providing a combined job hunter/hiring manager/employer overview. *Employer Survey* answers provide only a partial overview of some 40 questions asked, many of which provided multiple answers and handwritten responses. All survey responses are for the year 1994 unless otherwise indicated.

Job Hunter Survey Summary:
Average Time to Find a Job and Difficulty of Job Search

	1993	1994
Number of months to find a new job	7.7	6.24
Number of contacts to obtain interview	89	24.3
Number of contacts to obtain offer	192	121
Number of interviews per month	3.1	4.4
Number of interviews required to obtain offer	12.6	8.6

When job hunters were asked: Are you satisfied with your job search progress? Almost three-quarters of the respondents (72.5 percent) said no. The majority of job hunter respondents (66.2 percent) reported their searches more difficult than expected; 18.1 percent of those respondents reported substantial difficulty in their job search efforts. Nevertheless, these figures are a substantial improvement (23 percent) over difficulties job hunters reportedly faced in the 1993 survey.

Insights from the Job Hunter Survey

Reasons for Job Search Difficulties

Asked to name the most difficult aspect of their job search, the most common replies in 1993 were *waiting, lack of response, limited number of jobs or no jobs available, and negative employer attitudes.*

Positive Job Market Activity and Outplacement

On the positive side, almost 50 percent in 1993 reported having offers or pending offers and slightly more than the majority of respondents (54.3 percent) reported they had received some form of outplacement. Outplacement was effective according to 57 percent. A limited number (19 percent) reported internal outplacement effective.

Reasons for Job Search

Forty-eight percent of job hunters responding to the survey were unemployed, with 6 percent on notice of termination or layoff. Fifty-one percent were still employed while seeking a new job. Within the last two years 58 percent of those responding had changed jobs. Of those individuals unemployed, the reasons most frequently cited (listed in order of number of responses) were (1) plant moved (2) layoffs (3) downsizing.

Job Market Condition

Job hunters, in an assessment of available opportunities in their areas of skills/experience, expressed their perceptions of the job market with the following responses: ample opportunities (excellent job match)—7.14 percent; reasonable opportunities (good job match)—32.7 percent; very limited opportunities available—54.7 percent. At the time of survey calculations, approximately 33.3 percent of the respondents reported success in their job search efforts. It is interesting to note that a majority of job seekers in both 1993 and 1994 perceived a negative employer attitude in regard to hiring new employees—78 percent in 1993 and 68 percent in 1994.

Job Hunter Survival

Over half of the job seekers (56 percent) reported they were considering opportunities in areas other than their career field. Of those who had accepted new positions 21 percent had relocated.

Consulting and Temporary Work

Consulting/temporary work is becoming near mainstream for job hunters. Forty percent of the respondents were performing some form of consulting or temporary work. Of those, 79 percent had found consulting work and 21 percent had found temporary work. Of those accepting consulting work, 65 percent had found part-time consulting and 35 percent had found full-time consulting work.

New Trends In Job Salary Levels

Successful job hunters accepting new positions reported several significant new trends regarding the level of responsibilities and the salary accepted in comparison to their former position and salary level. (See Figure 3.1)

Of the respondents, 39.1 percent reported they accepted lower salary levels when accepting a new job. When these figures are combined with those reporting acceptance of equal salary (20 percent)

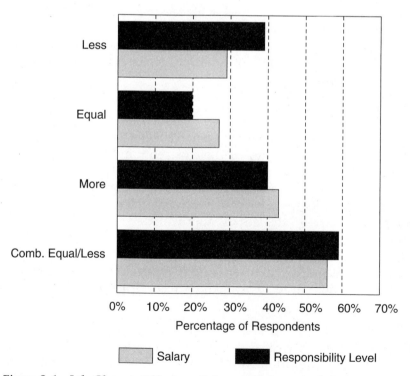

Figure 3.1 Job Change Effect on Salary and Responsibility Level.

the average becomes 59.7 percent for those accepting positions at an equal or lower salary. This is a significant downward trend (1993 was 45.8 percent), but as the job market improves these figures should also improve.

New Trends in Job Responsibility Levels

Respondents who reported they accepted less job responsibility—29.6 percent; equal responsibility—27.2 percent. When combined, these total 56 percent. While this figure has improved since 1993, it is still a significant change from past years. These trends are reflected also by the fact that two-thirds of survey respondents indicated employers tended to offer lesser salary levels than in previous years (67 percent), and 61 percent reported they have noticed a negative attitude by employers regarding the hiring of new employees.

Job Search Methods and Effectiveness

Job hunters were asked about the contact-activity level with employers during their job search. They were also asked to indicate and rank the response of employers to their job-search queries and their queries' effectiveness. In the sections following, you can see the top five methods used, a write-in response of the top nine most effective sources, and the top seven *least* effective sources of job leads/interviews.

Job Search Methods Reported Most Used

Job Search Method	Response Rank	Effectiveness Rank
1. Resume mailed	5	5
2. Advertising	3	2
3. Search Co. contacts	4	4
4. Company phone calls	2	3
5. Networking contacts	1	1

Number of Employer Contacts Made (Percentage Reported)

250 contacts—26.2 percent   50 contacts—14.9 percent
1000 contacts—25.8 percent   750 contacts—13.3 percent
100 contacts—19.7 percent

The Most Effective Sources of Job Leads/Interviews. Indicated by job hunters in written-response rank order:

- Networking
- Direct company contact
- Advertising
- Search
- Recruiters

- Professional/Trade Associations
- Other
- Referrals
- Agencies

The Least Effective Sources of Job Leads/Interviews. Indicated by job hunters in written–response rank order:

- Direct company contact
- Advertising
- Search
- Agencies

- Networking
- Recruiters
- Other

Discussions held with job hunters and a review of the survey data help explain the disparity between the high ranking of direct company contact and advertising on the most-effective list and its high ranking also on the least-effective list. Much of the cause of the least-effective ranking is indiscriminate answering of ads and broadcasting of resumes without good homework in matching skills to employer job requirements and needs. This condition is explained further in Chapter 9 with guidelines for job hunters to use in skills matching (the PEG Guide) to improve their ad-response effectiveness. In regard to the direct contacting of companies, job hunters should use the *99 Minute Formula* in Chapter 4 and the additional techniques and suggestions provided in Chapters 5 through 14.

Effective Company Contact Sources

The *Job Hunter Surveys* offer an interesting insight by job seekers as to what segment of a company's organization they felt was most responsive and effective to contact in their job-search efforts. Respondents' ranking indicated that out of six organization choices or combinations of choices, senior management was the most responsive and effective (43.8 percent); line management was next (27.8 percent); followed by corporate management (17.4 percent), human resources (excluding employment) (0.07 percent), and staff management (0.05 percent). The employment department was last.

These response figures are significant, indicating that the department with employment responsibilities is viewed by job hunters as being the least effective and responsive.

Financial and Related Data

Interesting additional results show that:

- 54.9 percent of *Job Hunter Survey* respondents utilized unemployment compensation.
- 69.6 percent reduced their standard of living.
- 37.8 percent sought additional assistance/income from other sources.
- 59.9 percent obtained professional guidance or job counseling.

Discrimination

Slightly more than one fourth (28.7 percent) reported they had experienced some form of discrimination in their job search.

Personal Traits for Job Search Success

Two key questions were asked regarding personal traits and suggestions. In responding to the questions regarding personal traits, job hunters listed one or several traits that contribute most to job-search success. These are ranked in order of the number of responses. Some 35 different answers were provided, but we have listed only those receiving multiple responses. The first two traits received an overwhelming response, and the following four an extensive response. Note, in some responses skill crept in as a trait.

- Persistence
- Positive attitude
- Flexibility
- Motivation
- Work ethic
- Determination
- Reputation
- Willing to learn
- Industry experience
- Marketing
- Presentation skill
- Organization
- Skill/Capability
- Stay focused
- Networking skill
- See opportunity
- Interpersonal skill
- Intelligence
- Interview skill
- High energy level
- Hard work

Insights from the Hiring Manager Survey

In interviewing job candidates, 42 percent of hiring managers indicated they were placing greater emphasis on a number of interview/selection criteria areas. *The particular areas of skill and experience where such emphasis is being placed today* (vs. prior years) are listed by hiring managers as:

- Computer skills (PC)
- Cross-functional skills
- Being a team player
- Being a risk taker
- Communication skills
- Sales ability

The hiring managers were asked *about obvious shortcomings observed with candidates today.* Answers are ranked in order. All skills reported were *poor* or *lack of skill* or trait.

- Communication skills
- Presentation skills
- Leadership
- Spotty job history
- Unrealistic expectations
- Assertiveness
- Cross-functional skills
- Negative attitude
- Job knowledge
- Management competency
- Transferable skills
- Social skills
- Appearance

Hiring managers were also asked to provide *suggestions to job hunters on how to better prepare themselves for today's challenging and competitive job market.* The top ten suggestions provided are listed here ranked in order. Many of the remaining suggestions are included at the end of each chapter.

- Be computer literate.
- Network, plus find and nourish mentors.
- Update skills, know the market, and keep current with it.
- Prepare for interviews.
    Learn how to sell yourself.
    Prepare for each interview.
    Sell your strengths.
    Work on communication skills.
    Display confidence during the interview.
    Put together the best possible resume.
- Research the hiring company.
- Be persistent; take the initiative.

- Target your market and don't waste time with indiscriminate mailing.
- Have a good track record.
- Have realistic expectations.
- Try different approaches.

Insights from the Employers Survey

New Business Strategy: Lean Operations Management

The *Employer Survey* results show that for the majority of employers (53.78 percent) the driving factor behind the general decrease in hiring is a business strategy for leaner organizations. It is interesting to note that for only 19.69 percent of employers the economic downturn is the reason for this strategy.

Additional indicators from employers show that a new mode of business operations has emerged and that 78.67 percent (up 10 percent from 1993) are maintaining leaner workforces to reduce operating costs. When you add in those who have only skeleton workforces (4.26 percent), the figure jumps to 82.93 percent—over three-fourths of employers operating in a lean workforce mode. To reduce payroll costs, 38.36 percent of employers are instituting some form of wage/salary freeze, reduction, or give back, delaying increases; or eliminating bonuses.

Hiring Activity

In the year to come hiring activity is expected to stay about the same for 46.44 percent of the surveyed employers (down 4 percent from 1993). A slight increase was predicted by 34.12 percent (up 5 percent from 1993), while 19.93 percent predicted a decrease. More than half of the employers surveyed (54.33 percent) could not predict when hiring activity would increase in their companies.

The key question for future job market conditions is: What percentage of eliminated positions will be reinstated when the economy improves?

Thirty-seven percent of employers indicated they expect to reinstate 25 percent or fewer of the positions eliminated. When you combine this response with that of the 51.14 percent who said none of the positions will be reinstated, you get 88.54 percent indicating very limited or no reinstatement of positions that were eliminated.

Employers were also asked what percentage of hiring they predicted for newly created jobs: 67.78 percent responded in the 1–25 percent category; 15.38 percent in the 26–50 percent category; and 15.81 percent responded in the remaining 3 categories (50 percent or more). These answers show the low level of hiring employers expect for newly created jobs in the coming year.

Hiring Attitudes

When it comes to adding staff, most employers are proceeding with caution. The 1993 survey showed that 84.42 percent of employers were more cautious now than in the '80s. The 1994 Survey question was rephrased to cover the previous three years, showing 63.49 percent as more cautious now, 7.21 percent less cautious, and 28.14 percent unchanged.

Recruiting Data: Trends and Impact

The *Employer Survey* points out a classic job market story based on the law of supply and demand and dramatized by the mismatch that occurs as the result of job market changes. Unfortunately for some job hunters, the mismatch hits hardest those who are forced into the market when there is an oversupply of talent and an undersupply of jobs available. For the employer, this is a scenario that allows the company to improve its operations with an abundance of talented, skilled, and experienced people on the job market. This job market advantage for employers comes with a heavy cost for many job hunters. The *Job Hunter Survey* showed 39.19 percent of respondents accepted new positions at less total compensation than received in their prior jobs, and 29.6 percent accepted jobs with less responsibility. Nevertheless, new directions in the economy can create opportunity.

Where the jobs are. Employers are having difficulty filling positions in at least a dozen areas. The skills in these fields are in demand. Our survey responses show employers have the greatest difficulty recruiting qualified candidates in these top 12 areas:

1. Management Information Systems (MIS)/software
2. Engineering/design
3. Sales
4. Other
5. Customer support/services.
6. Research/scientist
7. Accounting finance
8. Medical/RN
9. Marketing
10. Human resources
11. Environmental
12. Physical therapy

(Note that MIS/software and engineering received a substantially greater percentage of survey responses.)

Executive/Management needs remain slim. The decline in middle management positions and the low priority projected for these managers and executives is consistent with many other sources reported in recent years. It is also consistent with the current leaner organizations, flat organizational structures, and the participative management style adopted by some companies. Very few employers expect to recruit executives (2.97 percent) or managers (22.27 percent). In terms of difficulty, only 9.54 percent of respondents cited difficulty in recruiting executives, and only 28.14 percent reported difficulty in recruiting managerial level hires.

Employees also report a significant need for nonsupervisory professionals. The overwhelming majority (74.75 percent) of respondents indicate they expect to recruit in this area.

Surplus Areas/Difficult Areas To Find a Job. The top ten areas employers see having the greatest surplus are listed in order of response.

1. Recent graduates/business
2. Recent graduates/liberal arts
3. Accounting/finance
4. Human resources
5. Marketing
6. Sales
7. Recent graduates/technical
8. Customer service
9. Manufacturing
10. MIS

Job sources. The most effective types of recruiting sources for experienced hires are listed in order.

1. Ads
2. Employee referral
3. Contact/networking
4. In-house search
5. Contingency recruiting
6. Company recruiting
7. Retained search
8. Job fairs
9. Agencies
10. Target recruiting

Tougher Screening and Selection Procedures. Employers have modified their selection procedures to adapt to the changing workforce and business conditions. The top three selection procedures being used more are tougher screening standards, reference checking, and holding a greater number of interviews.

Special hiring incentives show downtrend. When asked what incentives were being used to attract desired candidates, 60.31 percent of the respondents reported they were not using incentives. This is a continuing trend away from the hiring bonus, although bonuses were still number one in the top five incentives (32.22 percent).

Quality of candidates. Employers were asked: "In general, how would you describe the quality of candidates?" In rating candidates as excellent, good, and fair in the categories of unsolicited, ad respondents, and prescreened referrals, the majority of answers showed in the fair to good column (1993 survey). Percentage-wise very few candidates showed in the excellent columns, (unsolicited 1.06, ad response 2.39, prescreened 22.1). A much higher percentage of job seekers *should show up* in the excellent category. In today's limited and tough job market this is a most telling sign. Job hunters today ought to be doing a much more effective job in presenting their skills and experience. Numerous other questions on the survey corroborate the quality rating. In the resume evaluation and candidate evaluation sections employers also see much room for improvement. You will find suggestions on how to improve the quality of your presentation and how to evaluate and pinpoint your background to specific employer needs in Chapters 6, 9, and 10.

Employer Comments

Following are additional employer comments from the 1993 survey to help you prepare for today's job market rather than the job market of the '80s.

Opportunities for qualified job hunters. Asked whether employers are seeing more or fewer qualified candidates than in the '80s, 66.57 percent stated more, 33.43 percent stated fewer. One-third of survey respondents report they are getting fewer qualified candidates than in the '80s! Thus, if you're a qualified job seeker, this is an opportune time to get your foot in the door.

Candidate shortcomings. Employer comments on what candidate shortcomings they most often observe in today's market are enlightening and are also supported by the *Hiring Managers Survey*. Ranked with the highest response rated first, they include:

1. Unrealistic expectations
2. Poor communication
3. Poor presentation
4. Spotty work history
5. Inadequate job knowledge
6. Unexplained gap in employment
7. Inadequate management competence
8. Poor leadership
9. Lack of social skills
10. Negative attitude
11. Lack of assertiveness
12. Inflexibility
13. Unsatisfactory references
14. Unkempt appearance

Preparing for today's job market. To better prepare yourself for the increasingly competitive and challenging job market, employers suggest you:

1. Do research and homework on a company.
2. Improve and increase your skills.
3. Be flexible.
4. Develop good communication and presentation skills.
5. Prepare and practice for your interview.
6. Know yourself and your skills.
7. Network.
8. Prepare your resume well.
9. Present a professional image.
10. Be positive and enthusiastic.

Survey responses to "How might a candidate increase the effectiveness of their resume contact?" are ranked in order:

1. Include a cover letter.
2. Address it to a specific individual.
3. Follow it up by phone.

Skills and experience in demand. Employers cited nine areas as being more in demand today than in the previous decade. As usual, these are ranked in order of response:

1. Personal computer skills
2. Industry-specific training
3. Participative management style
4. Hands-on experience
5. Visionary thinking
6. Innovative/risk-taking
7. Strategic planning
8. Cross-functional skills
9. Transferable skills

Resume Comments

The resume is a job hunter's standard form of introduction to an employer and the most accepted instant-screening tool used by employers. The 1993 survey responses offer useful insights into how your resume is measured.

Room for Improvement. Employers' overall impression of the quality of the resumes they receive (in terms of format, organization, and data provided) is excellent (0.77 percent), good (51.40 percent), fair (44.22 percent), and poor (3.60 percent). These ratings perhaps could be considered acceptable for a job hunter's market, but for today's employer's job market, they are very low. An excellent rating of less than 1 percent is a most telling sign to job hunters that they must do a much better job of quality resume presentation. Also, the fair rating of 44.22 percent is far too large. The preferred resume format, considered easiest to evaluate by employers, is discussed at length in Chapter 10.

Unsolicited Resumes. Unsolicited resumes get little response from employers. Seldom does the resume result in a telephone interview (82.31 percent) or a personal interview (81.3 percent). If the resume is referred to a line manager, the response rate improves: seldom 49.6 percent, sometimes 48.11 percent, and often 2.43 percent. No-interest letters are often sent (62.16 percent). Over half (58.87 percent) are held in a retrieval system.

Trends and Useful Data: The '90s vs. the '80s

A number of noteworthy comparison factors emerge from the 1993 and 1994 surveys.

Comparison of Candiates

	1993 Survey: '90s vs. '80s	1994 Survey: 3 Yr. Comparison (1991–1994)
More candidates unemployed 9 months or more	81.72%	68.75%
More applicants applying for lower level positions than previously held	79.17%	85.92%
More candidates referred through outplacement programs	Unreported	77.89%
Lower salary expectations	61.72%	55.5 %

In these surveys, job hunters, hiring managers and employers have volunteered substantial firsthand information on their recent experiences in the job market and the changes that are continuing to occur as we move into the 21st century.

SURVEY SUGGESTIONS

From Hiring Managers

- Be prepared for a long search.
- Put together the best possible resume.
- Be willing to relocate.

From Job Hunters

- Practice interview skills.
- Get help; don't get discouraged.
- Focus your efforts on networking.

4

The 99 Minute Formula

The *99 Minute Formula* strengthens job hunters' efforts to present themselves to and communicate with employers through resumes, letters, telephone contacts, and interviews. It involves all of the written, spoken, and other personal contacts made with employers and includes the necessary planning and homework required for a winning presentation. The formula is applied to three segments of the job search process:

1. Developing and gaining employer interest
2. Successful interviewing
3. Getting results—a job offer or other opportunities

In my years of experience as an executive search consultant, and previously as an operations manager and personnel manager, I have been fortunate to meet and work with thousands of job hunters, all essentially seeking the same goal: a better job or, for many, the ideal job. The hundreds of employers I have worked with were, in turn, seeking qualified employees to bring value and benefit to their organizations.

In working with the survey results, it became obvious that job hunters could gain substantially from the information provided in several key areas:

- Employer sourcing and research
- Job search preparation, methods, and techniques

43

- Knowledge of potential employer
- Presentation to employer

Now that you've read the results of the *Employer, Hiring Manager,* and *Job Hunter Surveys* in Chapter 3, you can see that survey answers emphasize job hunters' need to do a better job in presenting themselves to employers. In planning and overseeing surveys of the job market over the past ten years, I have observed a growing trend toward job hunters becoming lax in this area. The recent survey results clearly confirm these observations.

I remember a recent candidate by the name of Matt who I interviewed for a materials management position with a rather conservative *Fortune* 500 company. On the surface, Matt appeared well qualified with excellent degrees and solid experience suitable for the job. However, Matt's appearance was marginal and his resume and cover letter lacked a clear and concise description of his experience and showed only acceptable writing skills. Matt's presentation was friendly, but lacked enthusiasm. Matt also seemed overly concerned about work-rule issues. He asked about vacation time, if there was an on-site gym, if there were regular hours or could he come and go as he pleased, and if they had candy and soft drink machines on the premises. The total picture Matt presented was not sharp. Matt lost a probable job offer to a competitive candidate with a much sharper presentation and serious work ethic.

An additional factor gives great credence to the *Employer and Hiring Manager Survey* response regarding the need for job candidates to make better presentations. This factor, which I call the job hunter's *noncompetitive easy-sell factor* was called to my attention several years ago by a director of marketing who was being considered for a position as vice president in an internationally known materials company. The marketing director commented that since job hunters had become adjusted to looking for jobs in a job hunters' market—where employers were competing for their talent—they had become callous and sloppy (noncompetitive) in their job search efforts, approaches, and techniques. This was a very interesting insight, and one worth considering in light of the large number of job hunters struggling in today's lean job market. A pertinent question to ask is: Are some of today's job hunters struggling for this reason more than for a lack of appropriate skills or a lack of jobs? Certainly I have found a sizable number of job seekers who have been much more successful after honing their job search efforts and presentation.

All job hunters share a common thread in their job search—

making some form of presentation to the potential employer. The *99 Minute Formula* will help you put your job search in focus. It will help you package and present your skills and qualifications effectively. It involves the critical presentations you make to a potential employer and the period of time in which you establish a successful image. Here's a brief outline, which I will develop more fully throughout this chapter.

The 99 Minute Formula:

1. Developing and Gaining Employer Interest
    30 Seconds: The Magic Door Opener
        (a brief, concise, well-prepared resume and cover letter)
    5 Minutes: Your Personal Sales Opener
        (introductory employer conversation)
    25 Minutes: (Getting Smart)
        (preparation—learning about a prospective employer, its products and markets
2. Successful Interviewing
    3 Minutes: Your Initial Opening Impression
    5 Minutes: Chit chat to Build Rapport
    5 Minutes: Questions and Answers You Need to Know
    45 Minutes: Your Interview Presentation
    3 Minutes: Your Power Closing
3. Results: Job Offer or Other Opportunities
    30 Seconds: Positive Personal Wrap-up Note
    7 Minutes: Action, Closure, Offer, Other Opportunities

The *99 Minute Formula* will substantially help you in:

- Your spoken and written presentation
- Developing and gaining employer interest
- Successful interviewing
- Getting results

Most job hunters, whether employed or unemployed, share the desire to find the best opportunity they can as quickly and effectively as possible. That's why I designed the *99 Minute Formula*.

The 99 Minute Formula will guide you in the packaging and presentation of your skills, background, and experience. This is the crucial period of time when you either establish or fail to establish a successful image with your potential employer.

I have seen talented individuals miss out on job opportunities not because of a lack of capability or talent, but because of their poor presentation. Others have put this observation in a different light. They say job hunters don't take the time to identify their specific skills, strengths, and abilities, and they don't organize, package, and practice for an effective presentation. This creates what I often call the qualified-yet-never-a-winner -syndrome. Don't be a victim of this syndrome! Don't fail to make the employer winner's circle—the final candidate list—because you have not developed, effectively packaged, and delivered your presentation.

As we begin to review the *99 Minute Formula,* keep in mind this basic premise:

> Developing and enhancing communication and presentation skills are essential if a job hunter is to stand above the horde of competition in the job market. The *Surveys* bear this out. Presentation skills were at the top of the list of job hunters' major shortcomings in today's job market. Further, employers now more than ever consider the interview to be the essential hiring criteria. In most job searches all activity ultimately evolves through the interview, the key step to winning the ideal job.

Let's look at the *99 Minute Formula* in detail. In the following pages, each step is set out individually and includes both a recommendation for action and a warning on what to avoid. Some steps include references to later chapters in which the subject is reviewed in greater detail, providing additional tips and suggestions.

Developing and Gaining Employer Interest
30 Seconds: The Magic Door Opener

Thirty seconds is the average time shown by the *Employer Survey* an employer spends scanning a resume to decide whether the candidate is in or out of the running. This magic door opener is the time frame in which astute job hunters can set themselves apart and ahead of the competition. You can accomplish this by preparing a brief, neat, easy-to-read resume, one that is clear and concise, with proper grammar, and no typos. Your well-organized resume and cover letter must draw interest on the part of the reader so that you will receive a favorable response from the hiring party.

I highly recommend a one-page resume, with two pages being the maximum acceptable alternative. (See Chapter 10). Your resume needs focus—a clear, straightforward statement of experience and work history, background, skills, accomplishments, and objectives. (See Chapter 3 on why.) Include buzz words that relate to the employer's requirements and interests. This message must be consistent with your cover letter. Chapter 10 also provides thorough and detailed assistance in the drafting of your resume and cover letter.

Recommendation: One-page cover letter and resume. See Chapter 10.

Avoid: A resume over two pages, photographs, and cutesy material.

5 Minutes: Your Personal Sales Opener

Your initial introduction to an employer is your make-or-break time to gain interest. It generally involves your first conversation and/or your resume. It may be an introductory phone conversation before you send a resume, or a phone call to follow up on the resume you already sent. It could be a personal introduction, and in some cases it may be the start of an initial interview. It is the time when you— in most cases an unknown individual to the employer—have a grace period provided as a business courtesy in the introductory process. Take advantage of this time by being prepared with your best presentation effort.

Your Personal Sales Opener involves a brief, clear, concise verbal presentation of your skills, experience, background, accomplishments, education, training, etc. It is essentially the highlights of your career in a brief verbal presentation. It has great value in today's lean job market where many ideal job opportunities are not easy to find and need to be discovered and developed by personal phone call efforts. The importance of the introductory phone call and its format is covered in Chapter 10.

Your introduction is the first of four possible times you want to be sure to put your absolute best foot forward in gaining a favorable impression. The four times are listed here in the most probable priority of usage:

1. Follow-up resume call
2. Introductory phone call
3. Personal introduction
4. The interview

Recommendation: A well-planned, organized, and packaged verbal presentation (a verbal mini-resume), suitable for a five-minute telephone or personal introduction. It should be written out in advance and reworked until you feel it's 100 percent effective. (See Chapter 6 and 10.)

Avoid: Sounding rote. (See Chapter 10 on tone of voice.)

25 Minutes: Getting Smart

Preparation is absolutely essential. Appropriate preparation includes gathering information and making inquiry calls about the potential employer with whom you are interviewing. The *Employer Survey* (1993) confirms this point. When asked what suggestions they would give applicants to better prepare themselves for the increasingly competitive and challenging job market, employers answered:

> Job seekers need to possess more knowledge about the company interviewing them.

The astute job hunter prepares by gaining knowledge about the prospective employer, its products, organization, people, and marketplace. It doesn't take much time to find and gather such information; it is readily available from a variety of sources. The information you gain will help you respond intelligently to questions and comments about the company and its business. When combined with your presentation it will:

- Promote self-confidence during the interview
- Improve the interviewer's evaluation of you
- Enhance your probability of success
- Help provide you with a winning margin that many competitive job hunters will not possess

Many job hunters do not take the time and make the effort to gain such essential basic information. It is your gain if you do and other's loss if they do not.

Recommendation: Develop your job search plan with complete and thorough research and sourcing. (See Chapter 8.)

Avoid: The appearance of being uninformed by not having accurate data about your potential employer and the position being offered.

Successful Interviewing

3 Minutes: Your Initial Opening Impression

The beginning of the initial interview provides a few minutes of cordial first-impression time. If you are conscientious, well-prepared, attentive to interviewing etiquette, and careful to have an appropriate appearance, it's an excellent time for you to score lots of pluses and to gain an interviewer's positive reaction. For the unprepared job hunter who is lacking in knowledge, an acceptable appearance or interviewing etiquette, the initial minutes of an interview can be anywhere from nonproductive to disastrous. Various articles in recent years have indicated the importance of the first impression not only in the interview, but in other forms of social contact. My experience in dealing with employers upon whom a candidate fails to make a favorable first impression is that it can be very difficult for a candidate to reverse the impact of that failure.

Recommendation: Review, study, and analyze the first few minutes of your presentation. Plan it and practice it on several occasions. Adapt it to the potential employer you are interviewing and leave no stone unturned in making the best possible impression. Interviewers make offers to people they like, and certainly a favorable first impression improves a candidate's probability of being liked. (See Chapters 10 and 11.)

Avoid: A marginal, sloppy presentation; an unkept or radical appearance.

5 Minutes: Interview Chitchat to Build Rapport

The prepared job hunter who pays careful attention to the interviewer through keen observation, select questions, and astute chitchat will have a greater chance of becoming a viable candidate. Pay attention to the interviewer's interests. Clues may be available on a desktop, side table, or wall. Also note decorations and reading material. Other means for building rapport are areas of common interest, such as weather, sports, entertainment and world events. Additionally, you will find current news topics—particularly items you may have read or seen pertaining to the interviewer's company—appropriate for chitchat. Be cautious, though, about discussing government and politics.

Preparation provides tips on the company, its marketplace, products, people, organization, activities, and associations. Pay attention to the company's environment, its surroundings, its people and their style (i.e., environmentally aware or not, formal or informal, friendly or distant, casual dress or 3-piece suits, and so on). Your objective is to express interest and build some common ground that is not entirely related to formal job queries. In doing so, you will begin to build rapport and confidence as you proceed into the interview.

Recommendation: Be observant. Be quick. Choose topics that appear to be of interest to the interviewer. Be prepared to initiate and help carry the conversation. Keep to the mainstream. (See Chapters 10 and 11.)

Avoid: Being nosy or pushy and placing the interviewer on the defensive.

5 Minutes: Questions and Answers You Need to Know

Inquiries in the early interview stage regarding the position and company will help you zero in on the job, the employer's needs, and interview questions.

My years of experience in following up with applicants after their interviews indicate that job hunters consistently need to gather more information from interviews than employers provide. Many job hunters report interviewers cover a lot of areas without providing much detailed information, particularly in regard to the job. Yet, interestingly, many employers say candidates do not ask enough questions. Appropriate questions from the job hunter are effective tools in the interview and selection process. The *Employer Survey* highlights employers' keen interest in candidates who are informed about the potential employer interviewing them. Many times I have had hiring managers indicate they were expecting more questions from a candidate and often ranked a candidate lower in their evaluation for not asking relevant questions.

Appropriate questions regarding the job, required experience, responsibilities, placement in the organization and organizational structure help you develop responses to interview questions. Answers from the employer assist you in matching your particular skills, background, and experience to the position and company. To summarize:

- Questions help gather information to assist you during the interview so that you can provide appropriate skill, background and experience comparisons to the job.
- Questions help determine your level of interest and advise the employer accordingly. This allows you to learn of other potential opportunities.
- Intelligent, astute, and appropriate questions impress the interviewer.

If you observe that too many questions at the beginning of your interview adversely affect the building of rapport with the interviewer, then ask your questions at a time you feel is appropriate as the interview progresses.

Recommendation: Plan and develop some questions about the job and the company in advance of your interview. Role-playing before the interview is helpful in developing actual questions during the interview. In initial interviews try to gather enough information through questions and answers to determine your interest in, suitability for, and match with the job and the company. Listen to tone of voice and watch body language to determine the interviewer's reaction to you. (See Chapter 11.)

Avoid: Asking too many questions back to back, being overly aggressive.

45 Minutes: Your Interview Presentation

Employers in today's competitive world consider the interview to be the essential hiring criterion in their selection process. In most job searches, all activity ultimately evolves through the interview, the key step to winning the ideal job.

Nevertheless, the interview is the least practiced and prepared for step in the job hunting process. Lots of effort goes into preparing resumes and networking, but little effort goes into interview presentation skills. My own observations are borne out by the *Hiring Manager* and *Employer Surveys,* which show poor communication and presentation skills to be job hunters' leading shortcoming.

Many job hunters tell me that gaining knowledge of and mastering the interview process were among the most useful and effective new job hunting skills acquired during their search. Knowing how to package your skills and experience and present them effectively to match employer and job market needs will set your presentation apart from the competition.

A successful job interview involves at least six steps and often more. A job hunter interested in making a winning interview presentation should be prepared to follow all the steps outlined in Chapter 11. Also, a checklist to use in preparing for an interview is provided in Chapter 11. The presentation sections of Chapters 4, 9, and 10 also include items of critical importance in your interview presentation.

In Chapter Eleven you will also find the fundamentals of job interviewing explored along with the major evaluation factors employers utilize to judge you. To help job hunters successfully navigate the interview process, I provide four new guides to make interviewing easier, particularly for those who approach interviewing with trepidation and anxiety. They are the:

- Presentation Guide (verbal, written, and personal—VWP)
- Matching Guide (Position Employer Guide—PEG)
- Traditional, Nontraditional Guide (TNT)
- *99 Minute Formula*

Recommendation: Follow the *99 Minute Formula* outlined at the beginning of this chapter. Because of the importance placed on interviewing today by employers, be sure to read all chapters relating to interviewing (Chapters 11 through 13) as well as Chapter 6, which will show you the hidden keys to success.

Avoid: Being uninformed and unprepared for your interview.

3 Minutes: Power Closing

A solid close is important to an interviewer. It is the wrap-up on approximately an hour's conversation. You want to end your closing conversation with a succinct positive statement that summarizes your presentation and strong points related to both the position and the company. Essentially you are putting a focus on the many areas of your experience, background, and skills that were discussed along with the company needs during a lengthy conversation. The interviewer needs a solid understanding and quick summary or visualized picture of you to remember. Your image should be that of a successful individual with the skills, background, and experience to match the company needs.

I recall interviewing Joan for an important position with a computer company. The only thing Joan lacked was enough self-assurance to make continued eye contact, particularly when stressing a point and making a summation statement of her skills. Under interview stress, she tended to look away or at the floor. In addition, she sometimes hesitated for long periods of time before answering penetrating questions, giving the impression she was unsure of herself. Before sending Joan to be interviewed by the prospective employer, I had Joan practice looking into the eyes of her speaking partners and answering questions immediately. I encouraged her to practice this for a week with business associates, vendors, and customers. Joan's presentation improved dramatically, and although she was not hired by the employer I introduced her to, she did accept an offer with an excellent company several months later.

Your closing is like a gift-package wrapped for the best possible appeal. You want to wrap your summary in the most attractive presentation package possible to match the employer's requirements. Before your closing comments, ask the interviewer if his or her assessment of your strengths matches the company's needs. Generally, if there are skills or experience lacking, the interviewer may point them out. This gives you a chance to respond by describing experience or skills that may close the gap.

Finally, indicate your interest and express your desire for mutual interest. In doing so, you will probably receive or draw out a response from the interviewer as to their interest and the next step. Be convincing in matching the fit between your qualifications and the employer's requirements. Make the match up as described in Chapter 9 (PEG matching).

Recommendation: Be positive. Affirm your interest and your ability to perform the job and add value to the company. Attempt to draw out the employer's intent and interest. When no response occurs, use appropriate follow-up procedure. (See Chapter 13.)

Avoid: Leaving the interview without a positive closing and an inquiry as to the employer's interest and further action.

Results: Job Offer or Other Opportunities

30 Seconds: Positive Personal Note Wrap-up

As a courtesy, send a thank-you note expressing your interest and appreciation to the person who interviewed you. You should also thank the individual for their time and interest.

Be prompt in sending your response. Use it to indicate the key two or three points that highlight your capabilities for the position. Don't hesitate to mention any special abilities that are a real plus for the position and that may set you apart from and above your competition. Close with a positive expression of interest indicating you look forward to both hearing from the person and to the opportunity of working for the hiring person and company (use names).

Recommendation: Respond promptly with a one-page letter expressing interest and your ideal suitability for the position. (See Chapter 13.)

Avoid: Sending no follow-up letter or an incomplete one.

7 Minutes: Action, Closure, Offer, Other Opportunities

Follow up your personal thank-you note with a telephone call to express your appreciation and to pursue the opportunity of an offer or another suitable opportunity, if no interest was expressed. In the event you are contacted by the employer for more information (references or additional interviewing, for example) be ready to respond promptly. If strong interest has been expressed, be ready to respond to an offer. If interest is pending, attempt to gain information on the time frame and reasons. In maintaining your dialogue, steer the conversation to where you stand in the selection process. Ask if you can provide additional information. It will help close any gaps and cement your qualifications. Should no serious interest be expressed, be assertive in asking about other opportunities that may develop with the company.

Recommendation: Read Chapter 13 thoroughly. It provides details on closing, negotiating, evaluating, and improving the offer. Be prepared to respond in the following four areas:

- An offer
- Pending interest
- Future interest
- No interest

Avoid: Failure to follow up and to respond positively no matter what type of interest or lack of it is expressed.

With the *99 Minute Formula* presentation steps firmly in mind, you have now started the learning process on how to polish your skills in:

- Developing and gaining employer interest
- Successful interviewing
- Getting results

In the following chapters you will learn more about the job search process and winning job search presentations. Chapters 5 through 13 will take you through the job search process with each chapter sequentially laid out to cover one or more of the following subjects:

- Taking charge of your job search and getting organized
- Developing a job search plan
- Researching and sourcing potential jobs and employers
- Getting to know yourself—your skills and talents
- The employer's selection process
- Clues to how employers select new hires
- Winning job search techniques—marketing and selling yourself
- New guides for the job hunter
- Attracting and closing the job offer

I suggest you begin your own job search venture in the sequence presented here. Begin with Chapter 5, which will show you how to take charge of your job search.

SURVEY SUGGESTIONS

From Hiring Managers

- Prepare for the interview.
- Work on communication skills.
- Learn how to sell yourself.

From Job Hunters

- Target specific employers.
- Develop your resume with professional help.
- Maintain consistent energy and stay positive.

5

Taking Charge of Your Job Search

Most job hunters ask, "How do I effectively get started on my job search?" Experience has shown most people develop an acquired set of ideas on how to change jobs and seek a new job or career. These ideas generally reflect their past experiences in the job market, their past employers' hiring practices, and what they read—which is sometimes out-of-date and at times written by persons with minimal experience in the job market.

> Most ideas known to job hunters today were formed in a boom economy. The job hunting process needs a fresh perspective. What works today may be different from what worked before.

What was effective in the '80s, particularly what worked with personnel departments and hiring managers, does not necessarily work now.

Know Today's Job Market

Recent discussions with job hunters—along with surveys of job hunters, hiring managers, employment managers, and human resource executives—provide vital up-to-date information on *what's effective and working today*. Experience shows that there is no one correct way of job hunting, but there is a *job search process* that, if followed, will provide you with the tools necessary to obtain the ideal job. From this point, everything you read here will educate you on a job search process that works in today's market.

Your reasons for changing jobs will govern your approach and timing. You may be:

- Employed happily and just thinking it may be time to make a job change or career move
- Facing a potential layoff due to an acquisition, merger, restructuring, or downsizing
- Unemployed as a result of a lay-off, termination, plant closure, or move
- Facing a transfer and prefer not to move
- Unhappy and need a change
- Seeking a new challenge
- Unable to get along with your boss, arrange a satisfactory working relationship, or transfer to a better working environment
- Trying to broaden your experience
- Seeking a promotion and more responsibility
- Seeking a new career
- Unhappy with, or out of step with, your current company or superiors, their policies, and methods of management style

Whatever your reasons for changing jobs, the job search process is essentially the same. If you are unemployed or about to be unemployed, the critical factors for you are time and the loss of income. If these factors are in short supply, you must proceed full-speed ahead with the methods recommended here. In a down, lean, or recessionary job market you need to follow some of the nontraditional job hunting procedures suggested.

I'll never forget Susan. She called the president of each company on her target list. Susan said she was researching the biggest problem areas facing companies in this economy for an article in the business journal of the city where the company was located. A number of presidents she spoke with really gave her an earful.

Susan sent an individually tailored well-written cover letter and resume to every president with a problem she had the background and experience to help solve. Out of 29 letters sent, she received 5 interviews and 2 offers.

If you are employed and seeking a change, and expect to stay employed until you have selected the ideal job, you are fortunate to have time as your ally. If you are an in-demand job hunter or WOW candidate, you are most fortunate indeed to have both time and demand in your favor.

The in-demand job hunter is an executive, manager, or skilled individual who is often sought out by employers and executive search consultants. Walk on Water (WOW) candidates are individuals with excellent to superior capabilities. They often possess exceptional skills, and they meet and may exceed the employer's idea of the maximum company job requirements. They are always *in demand* and often require unique handling in the recruitment and selection process. Because they are sought out for their high-level skills and competence, they generally move to new assignments immediately. In-demand candidates often share some of the characteristics of WOW candidates. They have solid and often outstanding capabilities, but generally have not reached or been assessed as reaching the WOW level. They also rarely encounter any delay in a job move. Both categories are ideal targets for executive search, special assignment searches, or company in-house staff searches.

If you are in either category, you will still find value in 80 percent of the suggestions and techniques recommended here, even though you do not have to develop employer interest to the same extent as other job hunters, especially those who are unemployed. Should you, however, decide to broaden your job search interests beyond the employer who has searched you out, you will find the job search process most useful as well.

In today's job market, unless you are lucky, you can expect the job hunting process to take months. According to the *Job Hunter Surveys*, the average job search takes 6.24 months to be successful. For the in-demand individual, or a WOW candidate, the time obviously is shorter.

As you proceed keep in mind that the employment market today is behaving differently than that of the generally robust 1960–1990 growth period. In fact, the market may never be as active again. A recent Harvard University study concluded that "Unemployment today is much more likely to mean permanent job loss and that white collar workers are more vulnerable than at any time in the past 20 years."[1]

Keys to Finding the Job You Want

1. Know the job search process and how to develop a job search plan and execute it.

---

1. "Employment May Never Be the Same," *HRNEWS*, June 1992.

2. Locate the opportunity for a job by knowing the job market and working it thoroughly.
3. Make sure you are qualified for it with competent skills, background, and experience.
4. Present and sell yourself; show that you can add value.

You and Today's Job Market

To help shape your perspective on job market preparation keep in mind the facts of today's job market in relation to that of the last two growth decades.

1. Hundreds of thousands of middle management workers have been laid off.
2. White collar unemployment is up to 40 percent, from 24 percent in 1975.
3. More than one million workers have stopped looking for work, according to the U.S. Bureau of Labor Statistics.
4. As the U.S Defense economy demobilizes, defense jobs are down from 1.4 to 1.2 million and still free-falling.
5. Employers are operating lean and mean and more competitive with no quick return to the relaxed hiring practices of the past.
6. Economic growth is subdued.
7. Stringent business cost controls are in effect.
8. Employer hiring practices are more stringent and selective.
9. Government spending is tighter.
10. Hundreds of job applicants are competing with you.
11. Thousands of jobs have been eliminated, many never to return.
12. The unemployment rate in the last several years has ranged from 8.5 percent to 6.0 percent.

What a change in just a few years. In fact, just a few years ago, recruiters faced an almost impossible task of locating qualified candidates for some top management jobs. They also had difficulty filling some management, nonsupervisory professional, scientific, and engineering positions. Not so today. Let's look to the future for help in evaluating the changes. Despite a job market with a surplus of candidates for employers, some employment experts predict severe shortages of experienced executives and certain other professionals (scientific and engineering, in particular) throughout the '90s. However, with a new business era of limitations, a lean job market, fluctuating economic times, and the growing number of mergers, acquisitions, and downsizing, the picture keeps changing.

Fewer Jobs and More Job Hunters Mean Easier Employer Pickings

Compared to the booming '80s, far fewer companies are looking to recruit. The companies that are recruiting can afford to be considerably more selective. There is a larger pool of talent in the job market looking for jobs today. The recent U.S. economic recession has created a glut of out-of-work individuals including many mid- and upper-level managers and administrative support professionals. All this means many people are willing to accept lower-level jobs and pay cuts. In a large number of cases mid-level managers and professionals find it difficult to compete today, because more senior people with more experience and expertise are willing to take the mid-level positions available. Due to the large talent pool available, many companies are receiving an unprecedented number of unsolicited resumes.

Employers generally hold most of the cards when hiring. If the employer is unable to find the person wanted for a position, the job will likely be kept open until the right person comes along. In an employers' market with an abundance of candidates, many companies do not have to wait too long until the right person appears. The surplus job market has dealt employers a full house—an employers' market! It is important for today's job hunter to recognize and deal with this situation accordingly. As a result of this market, job candidates can expect tougher screening and additional skill requirements.

Job Hunters Need Multidimensional Skills

Only job hunters with current in-demand skills will stand out and be selected for serious consideration today. Individuals who can fully answer the employer's key questions, "What value can you add?" and "Why should I hire you?" are the individuals who will be hired. As a job seeker, you must practice a new art—winning out over your job competition. In addition, with fewer jobs available in many industries, some will find it necessary to acquire new skills to meet employers' needs.

If you have a good perspective on the job market and understand the dynamics of today's changing business world, you have taken an immense step in front of the individual who lacks this knowledge. If your perspective on the job market is up-to-date, you recognize the vast changes occurring and the increasing level of capability required by employers, you should be able to respond positively to the job market. If you can offer multiple skills, and particularly up-to-date skills, you will be more attractive than the person with one-dimensional or outdated skills. If you offer a positive attitude, you obviously offer more than the person who doesn't. And if you have the ability to solve problems, you will obviously get the nod over the individual who doesn't. If your presentation can convince an employer that you possess such knowledge and skills, particularly the multidimensional capabilities described earlier, you will really stand out when the big question is asked: "Why should I hire you?"

Changes Present Opportunities

We have seen a fundamental change in the U.S. job market in recent years. Opportunities are the by-product of change and upheaval. Those who are able to respond to change will be successful. Job opportunities in the mid-1990s are still around, but in fewer numbers. Job hunters will have to, in many cases, seek them out with an aggressive job search plan, applying all of the tools from the job search process outlined for you here.

In the last year or two, many job hunting candidates told us they perceived their job search as mildly difficult to somewhat difficult, and their expected time frame for the search was two to three months. Almost all found the job hunting task more difficult than expected. The surveys show, it takes the average job hunter more than six months to find a job.

One of America's leading business educators, Peter Drucker, sees the years ahead as rough ones—and an open challenge for those willing to respond to change. If you wishfully think the job market will return to the days of the roaring '70s and '80s, wish again. There is simply no major driving force to move the job market into high gear.

The Mid-1990s Job Market—a New Ball Game

Careers and jobs are no longer a lifetime commitment. Job talent is now as much governed by you as by your employer. In past years, improvement in an employee's job talents were often encouraged and pushed with employers being the motivating force. Today this is only partially true. You need to take charge of your career growth and skills progression to meet both employer and future job market needs.

Discussions with job applicants and a review of the surveys show that entrants into the job market today are facing increasing challenges never before experienced. Let's look quickly again at some of those mentioned in Chapter 3.

- Continuing job market condition of fewer jobs available
- Tremendous competition for jobs
- Lower salaries and less responsible jobs being offered; competitive/well qualified job hunters willing to take less money
- Employers more demanding and selective—more willing to wait for ideal candidate
- Upgraded qualifications/skills level required by employer
- Positions require more flexibility
- Hands-on management/work-style preferred
- Employers seeking more candidates with multidimensional skills
- Participative/team management ability desired
- More candidate competition with greater skill level

The global competitive game has begun and is well underway. It is not unusual today to have hundreds of people competing for individual jobs across a spectrum of industry and business. Like a trained athlete, each person seeking a new job has specific skills, capabilities, and interests to offer a future employer. Each individual should seek to stand out and become more competitive in a tougher U.S. market and in a more competitive and growing world economy. American job hunters must put forth their best efforts to match the changing requirements of business and industry in the global competitive game, as we move toward the the 21st century.

You have begun your job journey by examining the job market, its make-up, and topography. You have gained a perspective. Now you can move on. With sound help, solid planning, and strategic action you can use the forces of change to your benefit. While hundreds and perhaps thousands of job hunters are behind the times, you can prosper and succeed with the *99 Minute Formula* and the tools described in the remaining chapters.

Get Informed to Get Started

To understand what's happening in today's job market read applicable business news media. Ask lots of questions of people in business—hiring managers, senior managers, human resources managers, and those in the job placement industry—and particularly of senior managers in your field of experience and interest. The only excuse for not knowing what jobs are available and what's happening related to your skills and abilities is your lack of effort. Assertively working the behind-the-scenes and hidden job markets can make an important difference in the opportunities available to you. Don't ignore these markets!

The Job Search Process

Most successful job hunters indicate that while their job search was time-consuming and laborious, it was also a satisfying and enlightening process. You will find the following Ten Step Outline of the job search process useful in getting your job search started.

1. Thinking of changing jobs—the thought process before the decision.
2. Making the decision—voluntarily or involuntarily. Choose your time frame if you can, keep your cool, and master the job search process to your benefit.
3. Getting started and organized. Develop a format, plan, and action agenda. Set a work schedule that includes goals and objectives.
4. Getting informed—learn about the job market and yourself. Learn what's available, what's behind the scenes, what the hidden job market offers and how to develop job opportunities. (See Chapters 3, 8, and 10.)
5. Preparing your background, experience, and skills, for presentation—resume, letters, introductions, and so on. (See Chapters 9 and 10.)
6. Matching your talents, skills, and experience to the job market and preparing a job search plan. (See Chapters 8 and 9.)
7. Marketing and selling yourself to the job market. Contact potential employers, job leads, and target companies. Network. Develop job opportunities using known and to-be-developed unknown sources and contacts. Work all useful and effective avenues to potential employers. (See Chapters 7 through 9.)
8. Gaining employer interest in your presentation—initial

contact, introduction, telephone, resume, cover letter, and interviewing. (See Chapters 4 and 10.)

9. Completing the employer selection process—pending interest, offer, negotiating, closure, or other opportunities. (See Chapters 7, 11, 12, and 13.)

10. Starting a new job on the right foot—the end of the job search and a new beginning.

Know What's Happening and Act

Know the job market, its sources, and resources. Be informed about the job market and yourself. Know yourself, your talents, skills, abilities, and presentation style. Access the market and become a highly active player. Get to know the opportunities available both openly and behind the scenes. Who's hiring? Who's doing well? Who's in trouble and needs help? Know your competition and how you measure up. Develop your search plan. Market and sell yourself. Network, and work, and work, and work.

If you find you reach an impasse in your job search efforts, regroup, reevaluate, and—if additional help is required—seek guidance and assistance from professional counselors, associates, peers, and successful managers in your field. Some human resource executives and search consultants can be excellent sounding boards for guidance and assistance. If you find yourself struggling in your job search look more carefully at the behind-the-scenes and hidden job market for a variety of opportunities and career options.

For example, look at entrepreneurship, franchising, consulting, and recareering. If recareering is necessary, you will want to consider new job training, skills development, and education as soon as possible. Survey results and discussions with job hunters show that professionals are making such career transitions successfully. In Chapter 14, we'll look at recareering, entrepreneurship, franchising, and consulting as viable and positive alternatives for many job hunters. Chapter 14 also covers strategies for problems and special situations. The turbulent climate of the mid-1990s, with the vast changes that are occurring, can be overcome if you are willing to be flexible, adjust to the changes, and put in the extra efforts needed for a successful job change. Such efforts may include all or several of the following: increasing your skills level, better resourcing, good action planning, good presentation, and assertive marketing and selling of your talents.

The Bottom Line for Job Search Success

The bottom line for job search success is being informed. That means you must access the job market to learn where all the potential job opportunities exist or where they can be developed. This is vitally important and should be reviewed by any job hunter the moment the decision is made (or the employer makes the decision for the job hunter!) to look for a new job.

If you have time to prepare yourself for your job search before you jump into the job market, you will want to thoroughly work the job search process as outlined in this chapter and allow yourself time to complete your search in the most effective manner possible. If you do not have the luxury of time to work the entire job search process before entering the job market due to a layoff or similar situation, then you need to immediately move forward with your job search efforts, beginning with step 3—getting started and organized. If possible, simultaneously work in steps 4 and 5—getting informed and preparing your presentation. Do not pass over any of these steps lightly. At the same time, begin accessing the job market immediately to learn of all potential opportunities that exist or can be developed. Detailed comments, suggestions and tips for working the job search process and developing a job search plan are provided in Chapter 8.

Getting Organized and Getting Started

You need to get organized and properly set up to execute the multiple activities of an effective job search. According to many job hunters, in the final analysis it's how you organize and handle your job contacts and leads and how well you follow up on them that is the key to your job search success. A successful job hunt begins when a job hunter performs a number of mundane tasks to get the job search off the ground.

1. Getting organized:
    Set up a work area with appropriate equipment and materials.
    Establish a method of data information handling and presentation.
    Establish a method of research and sourcing.
    Establish a method of typing and presenting your material (typewriter, word processor, computer, outside services, or other).

2. Setting a workable schedule.
3. Developing a format and agenda to work with and for follow up.

Action Plan and Agenda

In getting organized, you will want to establish some realistic performance goals and objectives for your search effort, including an action agenda for implementing the job search process. Much of the success of your job search hinges upon your daily activities and the implementation of your search plan efforts, which include establishing a regular period for monitoring and reviewing your progress.

Calendars and Other Schedule Organizers

Many candidates indicate it is most helpful to develop a schedule and maintain a pace in their search. They recommend setting up a process to track their many contacts with their network and potential employers. A calendar can be a helpful tool in this process. Some job seekers have found it helpful to create special forms and a simple system for follow up purposes (see workbook offered on last page of book). This is essential when you have hundreds, perhaps thousands, of people with whom you need to maintain contact on a regular basis. Computer literacy and the use of a computer system becomes a very useful tool for your job search efforts, particularly when combined with the word processing and mail/merge capabilities available with current easy-to-use software.

Data Information Handling and Presentation

If you are computer literate, you will find the basic task of maintaining and recording information for your search much easier. If you are not computer literate or only partially so, this would be a good time for you to begin a training program to update your skills. Some candidates we know have become computer literate on their own without outside training; others we know have done so with minimal training. Still others have taken short intense sessions or evening classes and done well after four or five classes.

In seven recent searches we completed for major management positions—including chief operations officer, president, general manager, controller, director of engineering, operations manager and director of product/quality assurance—all required computer literate individuals with substantial personal computer skills. In each of these searches for senior managers, the employers involved were not willing to let the senior managers depend upon their subordinates for these skills. The real advantage of using a computer is combining its word processing capabilities with the ability to maintain substantial data that can be quickly retrieved on hundreds of companies, their executives, and related useful company, organization, product and/ or service information. The word processing capabilities of computers and printers for easily producing, amending, and changing letters and resumes for various jobs and employment opportunities will greatly enhance any job hunter's search efforts. In lieu of using a computer, three by five cards can be used and maintained in file boxes for manual retrieval, while using a typewriter or word processor for letters and resumes. In fact, you can proceed without a computer and typing skills by having your typing done by outside services, as people have done for many years. However, without a computer you do not have the ability to quickly store and retrieve employer sourcing material that you can use in phone calling, letter writing, and mailing.

Word processing or computer skills will allow you to respond immediately to the need of changing your letters and other material as necessary for your job market communications. The ability to tailor your cover letters to unique employer needs and to change or reformat your resume during the course of your job search may make the difference in receiving the offer you desire.

Establishing a Work Area for Your Search

In any good job search effort, you need a place that provides you with some peace and quiet, which you can use regularly for your review and analysis of your efforts as well as for a work area to maintain files, research and sourcing data, and your office equipment. Besides a typewriter, word processor or computer, a fax machine is helpful for research, sourcing, gathering data, and some inquiry contacts. It also allows you to communicate quickly with your network and sources and to receive quick responses from employers to your resume and other communications. It is important to designate a work space where you have regular use of a telephone, answering machine, storage space for your research and sourcing material (computer preferred) and space for effective organizing and research. It is psychologically very important for unemployed job hunters to designate a regular work schedule and work space for their job search efforts and that they regularly work from that area. If you have no area for work space, seek one out as best you can (such as working from an outplacement office). Successful job hunters tell me that working their search efforts on a continual basis was critical to their success.

Telephone and Answering Machine

Throughout your search efforts, a private line is needed that will be uninterrupted by lots of other nonrelated phone activity. An answering machine or voice mail system now offered by phone companies is most useful to receive messages. Your ability to receive messages is important and the quality and accuracy of your message is a very important part of your image. We have seen candidates who have missed out on interviews and offers because of the failure to receive messages or accurate information from messages left for them.

Computer or Workbook File System

Either a computer or a workbook file system is necessary to maintain your job source and other research material on employers, particularly your contact list with names and addresses. If you have a computer, be sure to consider the use of data banks, on-line services, and electronic mail access.

For those with a computer, a modem and appropriate computer skills, various job opening listings and job materials are available from numerous data bank and on-line services. Lists of companies by industry and product with key executives and contact data are also available. Access to this material will greatly expand your job search efforts. In addition, you may want to subscribe to one or more of these services, which are listed for you in the sourcing material in the appendix.

Typewriters and word processors start at about $200. A computer system starts at about $900. and goes up depending on accessories and capabilities.

Additional materials needed:

- Writing materials
- Research and sourcing file materials
- Stationery

Scheduling Goals

Whether you are employed or unemployed during your job search, the task of setting and scheduling realistic goals and objectives is not an easy one, but is necessary to keep you moving forward on your journey to a new job.

1. Set a realistic time frame to complete your job search. Base it on the experiences of others in the same or similar areas of background, skills, training, and expertise.
2. Develop a daily, weekly, and monthly job search plan or schedule.

If Unemployed

If you are unemployed you should be spending your full time looking for a job, a minimum of 40 hours a week. Don't waste time in your job search effort; time is critical and time is money. Mentally speaking, the longer it takes, the more difficult the task becomes. In today's job market, unless you are lucky, an in demand or a WOW candidate, you can expect the job hunting process to take months before you are successful. The *Job Hunters Surveys* show that the average job search takes 6.24 months. Hint: Don't fall for the tendency to take a lengthy vacation if you just have been or expect to be laid off. A few days break or a week off is a good change of pace, but we are told by many job hunters that anything more makes it more difficult to gain momentum in your job search.

If Employed and About to Be Unemployed

If you are employed and have given notice or are about to be let go, you should follow the same advice as that for unemployed job seekers.

If Employed

If you are employed, and have not given notice, and do not plan to do so until you have obtained another job, you're in an excellent position to take your time to schedule your job search. A solid rule to follow, if at all possible, is never quit a job until you have a new one. In most cases, if you quit your job, you have lost your bargaining power and the ability to negotiate the best possible salary offer.

As in any other business activity, getting started right is basic to getting the task accomplished. You must develop your own work schedule and review and monitor your progress.

To be successful, job hunting requires work and discipline. It may require extra discipline (more than you expect initially) to move forward, to get out into the world of business, and to contact the people who will respond to your talents, hopefully at the right time. If not at the right time or place, you must continue to work the process until you are at the right place at the right time.

SURVEY SUGGESTIONS

From Hiring Managers

- Try different approaches.
- Sell your strengths.
- Display confidence during the interview.

From Job Hunters

- Develop your network before deciding to make a change.
- Concentrate on who you know.
- Follow up on all leads.

6

The Hidden Keys to Job Search Success

In order to find the ideal job in today's job market, a personal self-assessment is essential. Comments from job hunters who have been successful reveal that getting a better job depends on the job seeker's ability to package their special talents and sell them to a potential employer. To do this effectively you must get to know yourself.

What You Must Know and Why

Ask yourself:

- Do I know all of my personal skills and talents?
- Can I quickly summarize my background, experience, accomplishments, and strengths?
- What are my interests, likes, dislikes, and preferences?
- What are my goals, objectives, and expectations?

Getting to know yourself is one of the most basic and vital elements of the whole job search process. Your own personal data base provides you with the basic self-assessment information needed to sell yourself to potential employers. In today's lean market you cannot afford to leave any stone unturned. If you leave any talents and capabilities unmentioned in interviews, you are shortchanging yourself.

Many job seekers have said that knowing their skills, talents and capabilities was the key that helped unlock the door to a larger world of job opportunities. To learn more about yourself, ask yourself the key question: Do I really know myself, all of my skills and talents? You may say, "Of course." But think again.

When was the last time you asked yourself if you like variety or are more comfortable with a set routine? If you prefer a set routine, you certainly wouldn't want to work in a network newsroom. On the other hand, if you like variety, you might well lose your mind if you were to take a job as a telephone operator. If you pass out at the sight of blood, by all means don't fill out an application to be a paramedic. If you were born with raw nerves, an air traffic controller position is not for you. Are you the curious sort? By all means, be a researcher, private investigator, or a diagnostician. If you avoid or prefer not to work with people, you should avoid working in sales or customer service.

In your effort to find the ideal job, it is very important to make sure that the job you choose matches the kind of person you are— your interests, skills, experience, and abilities. If you choose a job or profession to please someone else, in the end you will likely displease yourself and others as well. To illustrate this, I'll tell a true story.

A young woman who was obese and lonely latched on to a man of similar qualities. The computer was this man's ego, and through it he managed to rob a bank of millions. He was caught and sent to prison. While visiting him in prison, this young woman met and fell in love with a prisoner who was a doctor. In an attempt to solicit his attention, she lost weight and entered the medical field as a paramedic. But she had a loud, shrill voice with a bossy personality and made her fellow workers and many patients miserable. Eventually she moved and took a position at the county morgue. This was indeed an improvement, because at least she couldn't bother the patients. She certainly did not please the staff, however, and soon left her position there. She then became a receptionist in a doctor's office. Can you imagine! While there, she studied to become a lawyer in order to help the doctor she met in prison get out of prison. As a lawyer, she also created her share of problems. The last time I heard about her was in the *Los Angeles Times,* where she had won the distinction of receiving one of the largest legal ethics fine ever imposed in the State of California.

Knowing who you are allows you to know your:

- Strengths
- Weaknesses
- Attitude about work
- Job preferences
- Likes and dislikes

- Interests
- Skills and talents
- Personal traits
- Goals and objectives
- Expectations

Incorporate this information with your:

- Education
- Work history and experience

- Special training
- Accomplishments

The end result is a knowledgeable focused individual, someone who knows who they are, where they're going, and how to get there. Most important, they know what skills, experience, abilities, and talents they have to present to a prospective employer.

In some 30 years of dealing with job seekers at all levels, one fact constantly surfaces in comments from successful job hunters: Obtaining the ideal job depends upon the job seekers' ability to sell their talents and skills to the employer. Ask yourself if you would purchase anything major—an automobile, a home, or a computer, for instance—from a salesperson who was hesitant or unsure about his or her product. If this salesperson was vague about the product's history and performance, and in general didn't know its advantages, surely you would be inclined to look elsewhere for this merchandise. There are, of course, the rare exceptions of those so skilled they can bluff their way through any sale, whether it be selling iceboxes to North pole residents, or mink coats in the Sahara desert.

Unless you are one of this rare breed, you'll need to have the right questions and answers prepared for your interviews. Put yourself in your future employer's position. That employer will want to know what you can do and how well you are capable of performing. The answers to such questions must come from you, your resume, and your interviews, as well as from phone discussions that will occur and references you will provide. Knowing how to communicate and present your talents is essential if you want to get to first base in your search for the ideal job.

Obtaining the ideal job necessitates communicating to an employer what you are capable of doing and what you have successfully accomplished in the past. You will be judged on how you present this information in:

- Writing
- Interviews
- Telephone conversations
- The *image* you project

Many job seekers think of the first two points but seem to take their *image* for granted. This is a mistake, because if the image you project to an employer isn't a good match for the position and the company, your resume and your interview won't get you the job. Remember, creating your image starts with your resume and telephone conversation, continues throughout the interview and selection process, and doesn't end until your follow-up closing discussions.

If you're being considered for a position as director of protocol for the state of California, don't wear a seersucker suit with a flowered tie. If you do, no accomplishment, connection, or skill will be enough to overcome the lackluster social image you portray.

There are certain image faux pas, however, that can be overcome if you stay calm and think quickly. A woman I know worked for weeks to obtain an interview for the position of account supervisor on a major consumer products liquor account. Although well qualified, she looked young for her age. The president and the executive vice president of the advertising agency had greeted her and poured her a drink. As she reached for the glass, it slipped right through her fingers and onto a no-longer-perfectly white carpet. The president turned to the executive vice president and whispered, "She's probably too young to drink." Overhearing him, the woman stated, "I've been old enough to drink with your client's chairman and CEO, Mr. B., for years." The ad agency president quickly offered the woman another drink and the interview proceeded without further incident. Three weeks later, she was offered the position. A quick, attentive and appropriate response by the candidate turned a faux pas into a positive event, and the weeks of work to gain the interview were not wasted.

In discussions with many job seekers, I find many have been so busy working that they have had little time to spend on questions of self-assessment, such as what kind of job they really want and what their real skills, abilities, and talents have in common with their job preferences. You may want to discuss this subject with close business and professional associates, friends, a spouse, or others who know you well. Should you decide to seek professional counseling in the self-assessment process, be sure to seek a qualified professional.

While developing your interests, job preferences, and career plans, keep in mind that they will vary as conditions in your life change. If you have been laid off, for instance, your immediate need may be driven by the necessity to find a job ASAP to support yourself and others who are dependent on you. If you are in this situation, do not lose sight of your long-term goals; do not accept a marginal or lower-level position unless it becomes necessary to do so. The exception, of course, is economic necessity and/or a job that will attain your longer-term goals or one more suitable to your interests. In a lean competitive market it is important to be flexible and, most of all, to know your strengths and how to package and present them.

The Self-Assessment Process: 12 Steps

To perform your self-assessment, utilize the following 12 steps. The end result will be your own personal evaluation and database of total skills, experience, capabilities, and talents. You will want to identify all of the items described in steps 1 through 8. In step 9 you will complete your assessment outline. In steps 10 and 11, you will test your results and apply them to job market needs. For those who need extra help or assistance in the self-assessment process, step 12 provides for assistance.

Step 1: Decide what type of job you want; define your interests.

Step 2: Find job categories that match or relate to your interests.

Step 3: Identify your personal job satisfaction factors.

Step 4: Identify your strengths and weaknesses.

Step 5. Identify your skills and skill level.

Step 6: Identify your personal traits.

Step 7: Recognize your transferable skills.

Step 8: Identify your accomplishments.

Step 9: Create your personal assessment outline.

Step 10: Test your results and apply them to job market needs.

Step 11: Gather job information (a double check).

Step 12: Assess your skills and seek career counseling.

Step 1: Decide What Type of Job You Want; Define Your Interests

To ascertain what jobs tie into your interests first build a list of your interests, and then compare them to related job categories. The following sample list will serve as a starter.

Sample Job Interest List

- Business management
- Leadership
- Creative
- Athletics
- Sciences
- Human services
- Public relations

- Engineering
- Marketing/ sales
- Entertainment
- Computer/data services
- Teaching
- Health care
- Business services

Interest Questions

- How do your strong points (step 4) relate to the jobs that interest you?
- How do the jobs you pick utilize your abilities, training and experience?
- How do they relate to your career, work history and life experience?

To broaden your list you can review the Standard Industrial Classification (SIC) Manual published by the Federal Government and the *Dictionary of Occupational Titles*. Both can probably be found in your local library.[1] For reporting purposes, the U.S. Department of Labor divides occupations into 16 broad groups based on the SIC Manual. The Department of Labor also has identified the fastest growing and declining occupations for the years 1990–2005, and the results are available. (See the appendix.) Be sure to closely examine the growing and declining jobs and occupations as they relate to your particular interests. This representative sampling of interests is a starter list. When you finish your assessment, it will probably be very different in makeup.

---

1. *SIC Code Book*, Executive Office of Presidents, Office of Management and Budget, available from U.S. Department of Commerce; and the *Dictionary of Occupational Titles*, U.S. Department of Labor, Employment and Training Administration, available from U.S. Government Printing Office (see appendix).

Step 2: Find Job Categories that Match or Relate to Your Interests

Which job categories tie into and are suitable to your interests? If you are interested in accounting and finance, for example, or the field of human resources, you have a variety of job categories to consider. The following are representative of both fields but are not all inclusive:

Sample Professional Fields and Jobs within Fields

- Finance
    investment management
    tax accounting
    trust management
    auditing
    treasury
    risk management
- Accounting management
    general accounting
    cost accounting
    accounts receivable
    controller
    accounts payable
    payroll
    budget analyst/planning
    property
- Human resources management
    benefits/employee welfare
    recruitment/selection
    compensation
    labor relations
    employee relations
    safety
    training and development
    organizational planning

Develop your list from your particular areas of knowledge, experience, and training. Then enlarge your list from your research. In developing your list make several choices because you may, at a later date, lean toward one over another depending upon how the personal skills inventory you develop in Step 5 matches your primary job choice selection. In addition, positions developed for your list may need research on the qualifications or skills required before you settle on a job or job category that matches or relates to your interest.

Step 3: Identify Your Personal Job Satisfaction Factors

1. Develop a preference list for the tasks you enjoy doing.
2. List the working conditions and environment you prefer.
3. Develop a list of work situations that give you a real sense of satisfaction.

Possible entries on these lists include:

- Require unique skills
- Having change/variety
- Working with others
- Require competitive nature
- Managing others
- Performing repetitive work
- Intellectual achievement
- Entertaining atmosphere
- Opportunity to help others
- Contact with private sector
- Developmental/creative
- Status and attention
- Physically demanding
- Contact with public sector
- Working with things rather than people
- Variety
- Having power/authority
- Working by yourself
- Decision-making role
- Influencing others
- Geographic variety
- People contact
- Artistic achievement
- Exciting atmosphere
- Freedom/independence
- Work in pressured environment
- Flexible vs. rigid environment
- Secure environment
- Material need

Step 4: Identify Your Strengths and Weaknesses

Evaluate your strengths and weaknesses using the following as a sample to work with in building your own list.

Strength
- Efficient
- Risk-taker

Weakness
- Perfectionist
- Impulsive

- Tenacious
- Friendly
- Flexible
- Detail-oriented
- Quick learner
- Good teacher
- Good communicator
- Patient
- Assertive

- Overbearing
- Distant
- Inflexible
- Demanding
- Fade under pressure
- Poor verbal skills
- Poor writing skills
- Impatient
- Reticent

It is possible that a weakness in one work environment can be a strength in another. You may also discover that a weakness at times may be an excess of one of your strengths. Make sure you relate each characteristic to yourself carefully.

Step 5: Identify Your Skills and Skill Level

What are your skills and at what level are they? It is essential that you identify your skills and capabilities early on in your job search. This knowledge is absolutely necessary. You must know them so you can communicate them to your prospective employers. Your skills inventory will assist you in your job interest selection process as well. Following is a skills inventory sample list. Asterisks indicate skills reported as most commonly sought today.

Skills Inventory Sample List

- Industry specific skills*
- Managerial skills*
    - leadership*
    - problem-solving*
    - interpersonal*
    - planning*
    - risk-taking*
- Professional skills*
- Technical skills*
    - i.e., personal computer*
- Administrative skills
- Craft Skills
- Unique, innovative*, creative, visionary* skills
- Communication* and presentation skills*
- Cross-functional* and transferable skills (See Step 7.)

Remember to combine your skills with:

- Education
- Accomplishments
- Life experiences
- Hobbies

If an employer has difficulty determining your skills, you will not get an offer. An employer must have confidence in you and your abilities. Remember, it is up to you to communicate and convey what your strengths are in your presentation and to do so in a convincing manner. I have found that there is probably no factor more important in getting a job than a job hunter presenting an image that fulfills the employer's needs almost 100 percent. Candidates who lack a reasonable degree of insight into their skills and qualifications never make the finalist candidate list for the more responsible and higher-level positions.

Step 6: Identify Your Personal Traits

Hiring managers and employment personnel often call your personal traits the keys to success. They look for positive personal traits, particularly adaptive traits that allow you to make the transition from one company and position to another. These traits are many and all are important. Note them carefully. The following sample list will help you build your traits list.

Sample Personal Traits List

- Attitude
- Friendliness
- Motivation
- Demeanor
- Grooming
- Accepts responsibility
- Flexibility
- Leadership
- Ambition
- Punctuality
- Relating with others
- Work completion
- Sincerity
- Pride in work
- Dependability
- Presentation
- Enthusiasm
- Willingness to learn
- Patience
- Maturity
- Work ethic
- Honesty
- Listening
- Taking risks

There is a man I have kept track of with great curiosity over the years because his personal traits and work ethic are most interesting. He is a very talented and capable individual who works for a very conservative nine-to-five company. He works ten hour days and he works very hard, but to the extreme inconvenience of everyone who works with him. He has created his own hours: 11:45 A.M. to 10:30 P.M. with lunch from 2:15 to 3:00 P.M. He considers himself punctual because he works long hours, and he believes everyone he works with should be flexible enough to adapt their work schedule to his.

He considers himself dependable because he can be depended upon to arrive by 11:45 A.M. and can be found like clockwork at his desk when evening turns to night. His fashion preferences would be Auntie Mame's dream. He is particularly conscious of his grooming. When he doesn't wash his hair for days on end, he very thoughtfully covers it with a hat. People with all the right traits have come and they have gone. The company downsized, and there were massive layoffs. Through it all our man survived. It just goes to show that there are exceptions to the rules for talented people who are producers. And in case you want to ask, no, he is not anyone's relative. Subsequently, the company switched over to computers in 1989. As far as anyone knows, his computer has never been touched. It is a brand new four-year-old computer. One year his message box got so full that it jammed the system. Was our man reprimanded? Of course not. After all, it was not he who jammed his computer. He never even used it. Yes, there are always exceptions to the rule, but keep in mind that they are few and far between. In this case, the individual performance and positive personal traits far offset the negative ones for the company involved.

The new business world of the mid-1990s has created new requirements and demands on employees and job hunters throughout the country. Many well-qualified people are being forced to take alternative employment; others are changing careers. As new demands are made, many employed and some unemployed individuals are learning new skills with a positive attitude about change.

To accomplish a thorough job of self-assessment of your skills, abilities, and experience, you must maintain a positive attitude and not let a lean job market get you down. A negative or indifferent attitude is the kiss of death to a job seeker. Some people who have been hit particularly hard by the job market have sought guidance from a counselor, psychologist, or other qualified professional. Do whatever it takes to get on a positive track because that's half the battle.

Step 7: Recognize Your Transferable Skills

In the new and ever-changing job environment of the mid-1990s, the ability to transfer your skills and traits to other job areas opens up a whole new world of job opportunities. While new technology in such areas as electronics, communications, computers, word processing, testing, and automation has been responsible for eliminating many jobs, it has also created new jobs. Transferring your skills and traits to other job areas may be the answer for you, particularly if you are finding no jobs available in your current area.

Define your basic traits and abilities. Review your experience and specialized skills from your overall work experience and history. Reassess each of these components for a broader application in new or more diverse areas. The following brief sample list shows skills and traits that are transferable to many job areas. It will help you create a personalized list of other job areas where your skills and traits may apply. As you build your list, you will discover other transferable skills as well.

Transferable Skills List

- Managing
- Public speaking
- Administration
- Relating to others
- Leadership
- Selling
- Making decisions
- Encouraging/building
- Operating systems
- Handling information
- Presentation
- Solving problems
- Organizing
- Negotiating
- Analysis/evaluation
- Motivating others
- Planning
- Creativeness
- Decisiveness
- Teaching
- Writing
- Communication

Traits Applicable to Many Job Environments

- Resourcefulness
- Objectivity
- Reliability
- Sensitivity
- Decisiveness
- Results-oriented
- Persistence
- Tenaciousness
- Enthusiasm
- Honesty
- Adaptability
- Self-motivated
- Punctuality
- Competence

Step 8: Identify Your Accomplishments

Your accomplishments are very important to a prospective employer. They are proof of what you are capable of doing. They are a measure of your success and a yardstick for employers to judge your talents and future productivity.

Review your career and personal history back to your school days and develop a list of your accomplishments, including those for which you have not yet received recognition. Remember to include details such as:

- improved profit by 15 percent
- reduced expenses by 30 percent
- lead group to successive record-breaking performances
- achieved first successful program, plan, or test

Forms of Accomplishment

- Your accomplishments should include specific information, such as you improved something, saved time, money, etc.
- You achieved good or unusual results, beyond the norm.
- You contributed to a major change/achievement.
- You identified a problem and corrected it.
- You developed/contributed a new, unique, or noteworthy idea (patent, new system, approach, formula, process).
- You demonstrated leadership.

Accomplishments by Area

It is helpful to categorize your list of accomplishments by industry, management, function, technology, and discipline areas.

- Management accomplishments: reduced costs by 15 percent; improved sales by 15 percent
- Technology: developed new process, patent, design; improved yield
- Function: improved operations capability (describe)
- Finance: reduced expenses by 30 percent
- Customer relations: improved user application by 20 percent
- Human resources: reduced compensation claims by 33 percent
- Operations: improved production by 17 percent; reduced absenteeism by 14 percent
- Quality: improved yield by 31 percent

Type of Accomplishments

It is also helpful to categorize your accomplishments by type.

- Management
- Creative
- Sales/marketing
- Downsizing
- New business
- Improvements

- Operations
- Manufacturing
- Inventions/patents
- Restructuring
- Performance
- Reductions

To put a focus on your accomplishments keep in mind they are the result of a skill or a combination of skill, talent, and experience being applied to complete a special task or favorably resolve a problem in a noteworthy manner.

Step 9: Create Your Personal Assessment Outline

In completing your self-assessment, summarize the steps you have just finished. In the process, be sure you include a personal assessment of your career, work history, and life experiences encompassing your total skills and overall capabilities. An abbreviated summary outline looks like the following.

1. Job interests (type of job wanted, job categories of interest, personal job satisfaction factors, etc.)
2. Your skills, skill level, and special talents
3. Your personal traits
4. Your transferable skills
5. Your accomplishments
6. Your strengths and weaknesses
7. Your specialties, i.e., what you do best

Now go back to step 1 in the self-assessment process, and you will see that you have begun to answer or have answered the important questions in the process. Don't be resistant to review the 12 steps several times until you are confident you have completed each step. This will enable you to quickly answer all questions posed to you by potential employers without hesitation.

It is now time to ask yourself:

- What type of job do I want?
- Am I qualified for it?
- How do my skills relate to it?
- Do my strengths match this type of job? Can my weaknesses be improved or turned into strengths?
- What are my goals, objectives, and expectations?
- How will I communicate my skills and special talents to a potential employer? (See Chapters 9 and 10.)

Step 10: Test Your Results and Apply Them to Job Market Needs

This step involves testing the results of the self-assessment data you have pulled together to determine whether it is applicable to today's job market.

Ask yourself:

- Do my interests and skills apply to positions available today? Do they apply to growth areas or areas that are in decline?
- What is the availability of such positions? Are they in demand, difficult to find, or unavailable? (Check available job sources, such as agencies, search firms, advertisements, corporate postings, the behind-the-scenes and the hidden job market to ascertain numbers.)
- What is the demand for such positions in the future?
- What is the level of hiring activity for my various job interests and skills?
- Are my interests, skills, and goals realistic?
- If my talents are not in need or demand in today's job market, are they obsolete?
- If my skills and interests are obsolete in the current market, will need for my skills and interests reappear?
- If not, what skills are transferable? What new skills need to be learned?
- Do I need to develop new skills and interests based on current or new job market or employer requirements?
- What can I do to help myself achieve my objective of getting a better job in today's job market?
- Are there certain things I should change, add, eliminate, or avoid that would either help or hinder me in my job search efforts?

Step 11: Gather Job Information (a Double Check)

A useful method to help you finalize your self-assessment efforts involves gathering data using a variety of research techniques and sources. In this activity you can interview knowledgeable people in your areas of interest and skill, as well as read articles in the fields that interest you. By seeking out knowledgeable sources, you will gain valuable firsthand information from successful people who are where you want to be. You can also conduct informational interviews with employers and related professional associations, business groups, and organizations.

Careful research can help you avoid the often heard complaint: If only I had known before I took this job . . . The major plus for good research gathering is that you will develop many new job leads and sources, as well as valuable job and industry knowledge that will be useful to you in many ways (interviewing, leads, networking, cold contacts).

Step 12: Assess Your Skills and Seek Career Counseling

You may want to take advantage of vocational, aptitude, interest, and counseling services. This can be particularly helpful to individuals who find it difficult to define their interests and job objectives. These services can be a helpful turning point in discussing skills, interests, and capabilities and then aligning them to job market need. Be sure to ascertain the cost involved.

Outplacement firms may also help you. They provide access to a vast amount of job transition information. Outplacement firms are retained by employers. It is important to understand what services they provide, the skills level of the people involved, and how knowledgeable they are in your career and interest areas.

You may also be able to receive some advice and assistance from retained search consultants and contingency consultants. Keep in mind that retained search firms have their services paid for by companies who are attempting to fill specific positions. In a job market with an oversupply of candidates, search firms may be of limited help unless you are personally acquainted with a consultant or an associate, or your former employer can refer you on a personal basis. A firm may or may not have a person experienced in your area of interest, job, or market experience, but often can provide leads, general suggestions, and recommendations. Contingency firms may be more responsive to your inquiries, simply because they are paid a commission when they place an individual. Some deal in a form of modified retainer or expense arrangement with their client companies. We have not provided a list of job or career counselors simply because the numbers of individuals and organizations involved in such services are extensive. Furthermore it would be an almost impossible task to validate such services for recommendations.

Keep in mind that the intitals associated with counselor names (for example, John Jones, M.A. L.P.C.) may tell you nothing about the experience the individual has in job hunting, career counseling, the job market, and the associated problems experienced in getting a job search or career on track. Ask counselors what experience they have in dealing with problems in your areas of concern. Ask who they have worked with related to your concerns. Have they worked with outplacement groups? How many times have they changed jobs? Who have they worked with in their job counseling activities? Ask what organizations they are associated with. Have they worked with any self-help job groups or retraining/recareering groups? What job books have they read, and what is their knowledge of the job search process?

Completing the Self-Evaluation

Truly knowing yourself is a key to unlocking the doors to greater opportunity. Such knowledge combined with how you package and present your skills, experience, capabilities, and talent formulates an impression of you as an individual. It is this impression that will make a major difference in your success in capturing the ideal job.

SURVEY SUGGESTIONS

From Hiring Managers

- Know yourself.
- Know what you want.
- Keep a positive attitude.

From Job Hunters

- Timing is everything.
- Explore a career field change.
- Create a target company direct mail campaign.

7

Clues to How Employers Recruit and Select New Hires

Knowing the basics of an employer's recruitment and selection process helps the job hunter understand how employers select new hires. This means knowing what an employer goes through when seeking a new employee, starting with the initiation of a job opening, followed by recruiting, and ending with making an offer (which includes the terms of employment and start date).

A job hunter's introduction to the employer recruitment and selection process begins when employers initiate the recruitment process (ads, postings, word of mouth, employee referral), to attract candidates, or when job hunters trigger it through their own efforts by initiating employer interest. For most job hunters the introduction occurs in the employer's active recruitment stage through job sources used by the employer and job hunter. Following the recruitment and selection procedure described here, keep in mind how it relates to the sourcing opportunities available to a job hunter described in the job opening and recruitment process (eight stages described in Exhibit A in Chapter 8).

Recruitment

Recruitment is the process in which organizations find qualified people for a job opening and encourage them to become a candidate.

Knowing the sources that employers use to recruit new hires allows job hunters to contact prospective employers efficiently. The *Employer Survey* (see Chapter 3) describes the most effective recruitment sources employers have successfully used in the last two years.

In the list following, the most effective sources used by employers are marked with an asterisk. Bold print indicates those I have found to be most effective job sources in the last two years. Those followed by (JH) indicate sources reported most effective from the *Job Hunter Surveys.*

Recruitment Sources Employers Use to Find New Hires

- **Advertising*** (JH)
    Newspapers*, journals, throwaways
    Radio
    Professional, technical, industrial, and **trade publications**
    Product/technology advertising
- **Employee referrals***
- **Personal contact***
- **Networking/word of mouth*** (JH)
- **Target recruiting***
- **Direct mail inquiries***
- Hiring following temporary placements
- Job fairs *
- **Placement industry sources***
    Search companies, retained* (JH)
    Recruitment firms (expenses paid and/or quasi retained)
    Contingency search firms (employer fee paid when placement occurs)
    Placement agencies*
- Outplacement firms
- Open houses
- Universities/colleges*
    Campus recruiting
    College placement service
    College alumni association
    University faculty
- Electronic resume data banks
- Direct phone inquiries (JH)

- Government agencies
  State personnel employment service
  Related state and federal agencies plus job training programs
- Professional associations
- Trade associations
- Industry organizations/associations
- Newsletters
- Job postings
- **Research/direct sourcing***
- In-house
  Resume sourcing*
  Search*

Changes in Employer Job Source Usage

The following list from the *Employer Survey* shows those job applicant sources that have had a significant increase in use and those not used as extensively as in the past.

Usage Up
- Employee referrals
- In-house search
- Personal contacts
- Target recruiting
- Networking

Usage Down
- Retained search
- Contingency search
- Advertising
- Electronic resume banks
- Job Fairs
- Employment agencies
- Campus recruiting
- Government agency use

How You Can Use Recruitment Sources

Now ask yourself:

1. To what extent have I modified my use of recruiting sources to adapt to changing business needs?
2. What are my two or three most effective types of recruiting sources?

Many years of experience have shown that the aforementioned highlighted recruitment sources shown in bold print are the most effective. Keep in mind that the effectiveness of these sources will vary considerably depending upon the relationship of talent availability in the market to job market need. Even in an abundant job market, employers can experience difficulty in recruiting for positions that involve difficult or complex requirements or the employer may be looking for a WOW (Walk on Water) candidate superstar. There may also be a lack of willingness on the part of qualified talent to change positions or relocate. The effectiveness of some sources has changed due to the changing business world, economy, and job market. For example, companies on a long-term cost-cutting binge with an abundance of job applicants are not using outside placement industry sources to the extent they were being used prior to the 1990–91 recession as shown by the employer job source usage listings.

A job hunter named Larry, who came to see me recently, told me he found his first job through a personal contact at a local service club meeting. His second job materialized through a search firm, and his present job was obtained when he called the vice president of merchandising at a target company for whom he had always wanted to work. Larry believes it's not fate that determines job opportunities. It's hard work and a little luck in working potential opportunities, combined with timing and endeavoring to make the right match.

I believe Larry is right. Don't limit yourself to any one category, such as ads or search firms. Investigate all avenues of opportunity.

A note of caution here to job hunters as you evaluate the recruitment sources and their effectiveness. In recent years, I have been told by many job hunters that answering ads, i.e. sending resumes to search, contingency, and placement firms, and direct mailings to companies doesn't work. Most of these sources work, if used properly, and have been shown as workable and effective by the survey results.

Job hunters who respond to advertising with poor presentations will receive poor results. Job hunters who do an ineffective job of matching their qualifications to advertised jobs and to their potential employer list will also report poor results and frustration.

Job hunters who expect placement industry sources to be a magic source of jobs and to respond to their every inquiry will also be disappointed. Job placement industry sources are driven by employer needs, and when that need diminishes, so will the response to job hunters.

This is particularly true of search companies who are retained by the employer. These companies seek individuals who meet the specific qualifications of existing searches. Most are unable to respond to the large volume of job hunters who send resumes when their experience is not in the area of the company's assigned searches. Advertising, placement industry sources, and direct employer contacts, such as cold calls and target company mailings, are not ineffective if used properly. On the contrary, thousands of job hunters are using such sources effectively, as substantiated both in the *Job Hunter* and *Employer Surveys*. Job hunters will find many suggestions and tips to effectively work these sources and others in Chapter 4, Chapter 8, and the remaining chapters.

The Employer Selection Procedure

In the employer selection procedure an organization evaluates individuals and determines which it will hire as employees and which it will not hire.

Knowledge of the selection procedure will acquaint you with the steps that employers take to choose the individuals they desire. Knowing the steps in the selection procedure gives you an insight into the direction you must travel to be hired. This knowledge will enable you to adequately prepare and deal with each step successfully. The end result should be a job offer with appropriate working terms and conditions. An aware job hunter will learn to work the employer selection process as effectively as possible.

Make the Employer Selection Procedure Work for You

The selection procedure used by organizations can include anywhere from four to ten steps. In the following list, I have used an asterisk to mark the most common steps. As you review the selection procedure, note the number of times I have indicated a job candidate is required to provide some form of presentation—either verbal (V), written (W), or personal (P), as shown in the column on the right. A job hunter can be required to make a presentation from six to fifteen or more times in the process of convincing an employer that he or she is the right person for the job. As you review the selection steps list, keep in mind the number of times each *form* of presentation occurs, and that verbal (V) refers to all spoken presentation, written (W) refers to all written items submitted or completed, and personal (P) refers to all forms of nonverbal interview communication (body language, posture and carriage, facial expression, eye contact, demeanor, dress, grooming, and other physical elements).

Selection Steps	**Presentation Made**
1. Selection criteria factors established by job requirements*	
2. Initial screening*	
Resume/cover letter	(W)
Telephone	(V)
Screening interview	(VWP)
3. Interviews*	(VP)
Human resources staff*	(VP)
Hiring manager*	(VP)
Optional interviews	(VP)
Hiring manager's superior	(VP)
Peers	(VP)
Subordinates	(VP)
Work team members	(VP)
Application (here or Step 2)	(W)
4. Testing (optional)	(W)
5. References and other background checks	(VW)
Employer references*	
Education/degree*	
Personal references	
Other	
6. Additional assessment techniques (optional)	(VP)
7. Physical examination (optional)	(VP)
8. Selection decision*	
9. Development of offer, terms, and condition of employment*	(VP)
10. Offer extended,* accepted, revised or rejected*	(VW)
Starting date determined and arrangement made for relocation where required	

Step 1: The Job Opening

The selection procedure is initiated with a job description that includes at least some of the qualifications required. Generally, in most companies, it involves a written requisition to initiate action. In some companies, the written requisition or description may lag the approval process or the initiation of recruitment activities. In some smaller companies, no written requisition may be used.

The job description defines requirements, responsibilities, and qualifications. In some cases all the requirements are not listed, and in other cases the qualifications are not clearly defined. If this happens, it can complicate the selection procedure. (See Chapter 11 for a discussion of approaches job hunters can use when information on duties and background is missing.) Once a job description is completed and approved, an individual is selected by the organization to conduct the recruiting and selection process. Typically, a profile is developed. It defines basic areas of background, experience, education, special training, skills, accomplishments, special abilities, and other qualifications required for the position. (In the Workbook available (see last page of book), sample job profiles are provided for three actual positions: director of business development, president, and engineering manager.)

Knowing how a company selects its employees can help you work through the selection procedure. When you combine this with a knowledge of the position's requirements, the company's business, and its marketplace, products, or services, you will have a tremendous advantage in the selection process. The *Job Hunter Survey* bears this out. Accomplishing good basic research on a company before the interview stage builds confidence and helps you to respond to questions more effectively. As a job hunter you want to continually ask yourself how your skills, background, experience, education, and training apply or relate to the company requirements and selection procedure.

Step 2: Your Entry into the Employer's Selection Process

Initial Screening

The initial screening of a job applicant generally occurs in three ways:

1. When a resume or application is received
2. When an introductory phone call, personal introduction or discussion occurs
3. When an interview occurs (brief screening interview used by some companies)

The way you approach a company will have a substantial impact on whether you receive a positive response (request for interview) in the initial screening step of the selection process and, ultimately, in whether you achieve success in obtaining a job offer.

When a job hunter applies to a company for a position, generally the initial screening is performed by the human resources department. In smaller companies, divisions, or business units, it is often done by a hiring manager.

Most job hunters in business and the professions get involved with the selection procedure via the resume or resume/cover letter submittal. Some individuals experience the first screening/selection step through a telephone call that precedes the resume. In such cases, prospective employers ask the person's background and experience. In the professional, executive, managerial, and technical areas, relatively few candidates walk in to present themselves without a telephone call, letter/resume, or third-party introduction preceding their visit. At the nonprofessional level, many candidates walk in and are screened in a brief personal interview.

A resume, when not preceded by an introduction of some type, receives a cursory review (30 seconds) as the initial screening step in the selection procedure. In the '80s, when the economy was booming and there was a shortage of qualified talent, this resume introduction worked effectively for many job hunters. However, in a lean or down economy, and in an employers' market, a cold or poorly presented unsolicited resume introduction is seldom effective. This is particularly true when the resume is not preceded by research about the company and an inquiry call to ascertain the name of the individual to whom you should address your resume.

The Best Methods to Gain Employer Interest

In today's lean job market, the aware job hunter will prepare for an introduction to the company with appropriate research and inquiry calls. This was continually stressed in the survey responses to several questions posed to hiring managers and employers. The aware job hunter will either obtain a telephone or personal introduction, or the name of an individual to contact in an area of the company that relates to their interest, qualifications, and the employer's job recruitment need. The personal introduction to the hiring manager obviously is the most effective entry. An introduction to any individuals who know and work with the hiring manager is generally more effective than a cold letter to the hiring manager and the company.

The next most favorable introduction is to the person doing the screening for the hiring manager.

In many companies, particularly mid-to-large size organizations, the initial applicant screening is done by a staff member of the human resources department. The staff member may or may not have met with the hiring manager and therefore may not be thoroughly acquainted with the requirements of the position. Staff members not thoroughly acquainted with the position and the qualifications involved may do a sloppy job of screening. If this is the case, you must contact the hiring manager or someone more informed to make sure that you have all the information you need.

In smaller companies, the initial screening is sometimes handled by the hiring manager. In other cases, the initial screening is handled by a staff, line, or off-site human resources person. Keep in mind that hiring managers are the most effective people to contact. They are the most interested and knowledgeable individual in the entire selection process. In larger companies, if you are unable to gain personal entry or introduction to this individual, contact a subordinate in the hiring manager's organization, a staff person, or a peer, as well as the person performing the screening. Should no success occur with your introductory inquiries, a personal letter and resume sent to the hiring manager is generally more effective than one addressed to the human resources department.

Employer Evaluation, Selection, and Hiring Factors

The qualifications for which an applicant is evaluated in the selection process is generally determined by the hiring manager, often with the concurrence of the hiring manager's superior. In some companies, the human resources department will provide input for the selection process. In many companies, it provides guidelines for meeting the employer's legal requirements. These include federal and state laws, the Civil Rights Act, the Age Discrimination in Employment Act, the Americans with Disabilities Act, and other laws.

All job hunters should be aware of the major federal government regulations affecting them in the employer selection procedure and hiring process. Three federal government agencies and the Equal Employment Opportunity Commission (EEOC) issued the Uniform Guidelines on Employer Selection Procedures in 1978. We will talk more about these regulations in Chapter 14.

Candidates are judged on a variety of dimensions, some readily measurable and definable—schooling, years of experience, specific work history, industry experience—some personal and subjective—leadership ability or potential, ability to relate, and cultural fit. Keep in mind that most job requirements involve many such factors, which can vary greatly from industry to industry, and even within a specific industry. These variations depend upon the uniqueness of the company business, its marketplace, products or services.

While job requirements vary from industry to industry, the common evaluation criteria factors used in the selection process are:

- Skills
- Job stability
- Experience level
- Special talents
- Work history
- Accomplishments
- Values and judgment

- Schooling and training
- Presentation
    Verbal
    Written
    Personal
- Related interests/activities
- Suitability to company

Step 3: Interviewing

Employers consider interviewing the key step in the selection process. (See Chapter 11.) Interviews may be completed in one step with some companies; with other companies interviews may occur several times during the selection procedure. The initial interview may be only a brief screening or it may involve a full hour's time. Interviewing generally starts with a brief initial screening period (human resource or hiring manager or a designate) and is followed at the same time or later (depending upon the process used) by a lengthier interview by one or several individuals, depending upon the size of the company and the extent of the selection process. Further interviews may occur with the hiring manager and the hiring manager's superior, other department managers or peers, subordinates, work team members or other work groups. A final interview may occur during which the offer may be extended. Caution should be used by job hunters in the final interview stage who have been lead to believe they will receive an offer. I have seen companies decide to make an offer during the final interview, then as a result of further input, decide not to make the offer.

In some companies, particularly where the first interview session did not include the hiring manager, applicants are required to complete a second round of interviews. Additional interviews may be desired with other individuals, or second interviews may be desired with individuals previously interviewed. Applicants who successfully meet specific selection criteria requirements and are not screened out in the first round may be required by some companies to complete several rounds of interviews. The specific steps will greatly depend upon the company's selection procedure methods and level of sophistication.

With the advent of total quality management and participative management, many companies are conducting more interviews today in an effort to select the most appropriate and skilled individual for both position and company. The end result is that companies are striving for a higher quality workforce.

As you prepare yourself for the screening and interview steps, keep in mind that you will be evaluated on an objective basis (years of experience, education, degree) as well as on a subjective basis (ability to fit into the organization). You will also be evaluated on intangible factors—enthusiasm, interest, and motivation. In some job interviews, the intangible factors play a significant role, at least equal to background, experience, and schooling. Subjective judgments also significantly shape an interviewer's evaluation. Therefore, in your closing segment, run a reality check with an interviewer to make sure the interviewer has not gained any major misconceptions that you will want to correct or attempt to realign.

Step 4: Testing

Testing is an optional step used by employers to measure candidates beyond the interview process in a more objective manner. It can take many forms, from typing or computer usage to intelligence or aptitude tests.

Testing was more popular in the past, with its use waning through the mid-1980s. Its use has picked up somewhat since then and can be expected to increase again in the labor market of available candidates. The use of testing decreased in part due to the need to validate the effectiveness of testing, particularly in establishing a relationship to job performance.

Step 5: Reference and Other Background Checks

The vast majority of employers consider reference checking a vital step in the selection process. It is a method that uses prior employers to verify your background, work history, and dates of employment as well as to obtain comments regarding your performance, skills, and capabilities. Reference checks with current or former employers involve those individuals for whom you have worked. In many cases they will also involve those you have worked with other than your superiors. The following is a typical list of those references most often checked by prospective employers.

- Former boss (current superior if applicant approved)
- Former superiors in previous companies
- Human Resources Department
- Subordinates, peers
- Fellow employees
- Vendors, clients, and consultants

Be prepared with a carefully chosen list of references made available only upon request. Employed individuals should be very specific with potential employers regarding contact with a current employer for references. If your leaving is confidential, ask the potential employer to protect your confidentiality. Request that no contact be made without your prior approval. The same holds true for any additional reference you give that could lead back to your current employer (vendors and customers, for example). In choosing references, take time to contact each individual and advise them of your interest in them serving as a reference. Get to know something about your reference before you pass on their name. Ask your references if they are comfortable in being used as such. If so, use them only upon request from a prospective employer.

It is also important to make sure that you know your references as individuals aside from the fact that they generally may give a good reference or a good impression. John gave his boss as a reference because they got along very well. Moreover, John's boss knew he was looking for a better opportunity because his job was a dead end. Unfortunately, John didn't take into consideration that his boss often had numerous drinks at lunch or after work. One day John's boss told him someone had called early the evening before about a reference, but he couldn't remember who it was or what they had discussed. John did not receive the job offer, but at least he did learn from his mistake and that's progress!

Reference checking is also performed to verify schooling, major, and degrees. Some companies also require personal references from friends, business or professional associates, community associates, and leaders.

Credit and security checks may be conducted. Certain positions require additional reference checking. This happens in cases where an individual deals in special areas (financial, fiduciary, medical, pharmaceutical, security and others.) The law generally requires you to be notified regarding reference checks in such areas as government security, credit, driving record, and convictions. Laws on these subjects vary from state to state.

Step 6: Additional Assessment Techniques

Most job hunters are not involved in the psychological profile evaluation step because its use is not widespread. It is used sparingly in certain management, executive, and professional positions. Candidates who are involved in its use should ask the company to share the results with them. Other formal assessment techniques may involve a problem-solving session, a sample presentation, or other situations.

Step 7: Physical Examination

For a variety of reasons, many employers require physical examinations. Some companies do not require examinations at all and some are very cursory. Examinations should only occur after an offer has been extended. From time to time, we see candidates who express substantial anxiety regarding the physical examination. Unless a candidate has something serious to hide, the physical examination should not be of concern. I have witnessed a number of instances where candidates have been advised of a medical condition that should be corrected and all were accepted for employment. In at least five cases, I have had candidates advised of conditions that probably saved their lives or substantially prolonged their lifespan.

Step 8: Selection Decision

The decision to make an offer generally rests in the hands of the hiring manager. If others are involved in the selection process, the hiring manager most often will confer with them.

The decision-making process can be very simple in some companies and very complex in others, depending upon the nature of the job, level of position, extent of responsibility, and extent of organization involvement.

Companies tend to gather information for a decision from the whole selection process. In addition, the employer may obtain information regarding the applicant from areas unknown to the applicant.

Step 9: Development of Offer

Once the decision to make an offer has occurred, the company will evaluate the individual in regard to the level of salary/compensation to offer, level and extent of responsibility, fringe benefits, and so on. In many companies the development of the offer is a shared responsibility between numerous departments involving, most often, the hiring manager and the human resources department. In some companies the decision is left entirely to the hiring manager and his or her organization. It is standard practice for most organizations to weigh the offer heavily in regard to internal compensation considerations and to evaluate external considerations as well, such as comparative industry job rates, norms, and averages.

Step 10: Offer Extended

Once an offer is finalized it is generally extended by the human resources department. In smaller companies, it may be extended by the hiring manager or a designate.

You should request a written confirmation of any offer you receive. The letter should indicate the position, salary, bonus, stock, and any other special compensation items the offer includes. The letter should also confirm moving and relocation reimbursement if they are provided, the starting date, any special offer items made, and any benefits not included in a copy of the company's benefit brochure or booklet. (See Chapter 13 for further information on the offer letter.)

When your job offer arrives, take time to celebrate your success in making it happen!

SURVEY SUGGESTIONS

From Hiring Managers

- There are no rules.
- Match your skills to job requirements.
- Be specific about your value to the company.

From Job Hunters

- Develop an aggressive plan and stick to it.
- Respond only to ads for which you qualify.
- Obtain appropriate employer directories.

8

Winning Job Search Techniques

In today's job market good jobs are available, but to a much lesser extent than in previous years. Many of these jobs have to be ferreted out by job hunters because they are not as openly listed as in prior years. Companies have plenty of candidates available for most positions. They do not need to advertise as extensively or use many of the job sources of the past when candidates were more difficult to find. Nowadays, it is not unusual for companies to have hundreds of candidates competing for positions, and this condition is likely to continue for several years more.

Some job categories (staff positions and midlevel management, for example) have been cut drastically. Other categories (administrative assistants and group vice presidents, for example) have practically disappeared.

Know the Job Market and Develop Your Own Job Search Plan

The next step you want to take in your job search is to get a handle on the job market so you can effectively develop and execute your job search plan. Ask yourself the following questions:

1. What are the opportunities for a person with my skills, experience, and capabilities?

105

2. What major changes have occurred in the job market that affect the demand for my particular skills and experience?

The answers to these questions will allow you to adapt your job search approach to today's market and serve as a foundation for your job search plan, beginning with job source areas and avenues of opportunity to employers. (Note: A job search plan is outlined at the end of the chapter, and a detailed breakdown is available in the separate workbook.)

You become an aware job hunter by knowing what's going on in the job market, what sources are effective to use, and what changes are occurring, particularly in relation to your skills and experience. You may need to realign your interests and direction in order to widen your job search and attract the type of offer that will satisfy you. You will probably need to improve your existing skills and, in some cases, develop new ones. Rather than viewing such change as adversity, accept the change as a challenge and turn what might have been adversity into an opportunity for growth.

As you begin your job search, you will want to determine as quickly as possible what is available in the job market for your skills, experience, and abilities. Some job seekers will be startled to discover that no opportunities are available in their area of skills and experience. Recareering is the answer for these people. For others, self-employment, franchising, network marketing, or entrepreneurship may be a better choice. Others will benefit by pursuing the behind-the-scenes job market and the hidden job market. In these areas, job opportunities can be developed that are not visible or overtly available on the market.

Job Source Areas and Avenues

Most job openings and opportunities occur in the following four basic areas of the employer job opening and recruitment process:

- Visible/openly available positions

  Positions available through ads, posted listings, recruiting firms, agencies, employee referrals, word of mouth, etc., and sometimes through executive search firms when such positions are not confidential. (See Exhibit A—Job Opening and Recruitment Process, last four stages.)

Exhibit A: Job Opening and Recruitment Process

Stage	Action (By Employer)	Status (Formal)
BEHIND-THE-SCENES OPPORTUNITIES		
1. Thinking stage	No action	No opening
2. Discussion	No action	No opening
3. Apparent need	No action or confidential action	No opening
Action pending	A few insiders may know aside from hiring manager	
4. Position need determined	Limited number of insiders know	No opening
POSITIONS KNOWN TO BE AVAILABLE		
5. Need defined	Requisition developed	Job pending
Job opened and formalized	More insiders know	Job open
6. No active external recruiting except word-of-mouth or confidential search	Requisition; announcement posted; no to minor job action Many insiders may know	Job open
7. Active recruiting	Effort made to advise all insiders and gain employee referrals; normal recruiting channels used	Job open
8. Very active recruiting	Effort made to maximize recruiting sources; extensive recruiting	Job open

- Behind-the-scenes opportunities

  A position in the possible-development stage, thinking stage, or in the process of being developed and approved. No formal opening exists and no job requisition may exist or be in process; however a job may be in a developmental process. (See Exhibit A, first four stages.)

- Hidden job market opportunities

  A position available on a very limited basis, either through internal search by the company or through external search means. Searches may initially be hidden and later become openly available and may appear anywhere from step three forward. (see Exhibit A).

- Potential job opportunities

  Creating need by developing employer interest and showing you can add value to company. (Occurs in any stage in Exhibit A.)

Through studying and research, aware job hunters can uncover job opportunities that many other job hunters never see, thereby creating a much less competitive environment for themselves. It has often been said that over 50 percent of the jobs available do not enter the very active recruiting phase. In the current job market with its surplus of candidates, this figure may be much higher.

In a tight labor market, nontraditional job search methods are a must if you are to discover as many job opportunities as possible. You will need to target every employer you feel will have a need for your talents. This includes employers in related areas who might have opportunities available. Once you have targeted the employers of interest to you, including all the traditional and nontraditional job sources, you can begin the employer contact phase of your search—assuming your presentation efforts (resume, cover letter, presentation skills)—are ready to go, and your search plan and organizational efforts are in order.

Working Today's Job Market

The Key Factors and How Long It Takes

Until the early '90s recession, the average executive, manager, or professional generally spent two to five months finding a job, according to the U.S. Department of Labor. Today the average length of time has dramatically increased to an average of 6.24 months, according to the 1994 *Job Hunter Survey*. This is due to higher unemployment and the many changes we have discussed in the new business era of the '90s. The length of time it takes to find a job varies tremendously among individuals and depends upon a wide variety of the following factors:

- Job market demand/available positions
- Ability of job hunter to match skills to job market needs
- Ability of job hunter with unneeded skills to meet skill levels required, or to recareer
- Job hunter's level of skills and experience
- Assertiveness of job hunter
- Knowledge of job market and extent of job market research and sourcing
- Amount of time spent actively looking for work
- Quality of job hunter's presentation
    Resume
    Telephone skills
    Interviewing skills
    Personal appearance
- Job hunter's skill level in applying effective job search methods

I have seen a substantial number of qualified people work the job market very hard for many months, even a year or more, without success. The reasons for such difficulty can be complex. In my experience with job hunters, I have found that an alarming number have failed to adequately evaluate their skill level and/or perform a thorough self-assessment of their skills in relation to today's job market requirements. Many want to avoid spending the time and effort to upgrade or develop new skills, but they are only putting off the inevitable. Many fail to adequately develop an effective search plan, do haphazard networking, or deliver poor presentations. The process of upgrading skills, sizing up the job market, and executing an effective search plan is a continuous one. In recent years, I have found many job hunters do not spend enough time and effort in working today's lean job market. As a result, their job search often runs longer, sometimes much longer, than desired.

Work All Avenues of Opportunity and Forget Generalizations

In talking with many job hunters over the last several years, one fact clearly stands out: You must forget all the generalizations made about looking for a job. The *Job Hunter* and *Employer Surveys* clearly back up this conclusion. Note the following examples:

- *Never answer an ad.* Ridiculous! Both the surveys clearly show that answering ads is extremely effective if done selectively by matching experience to job requirements.
- *You can't find a job through a search firm or an agency.* Again, as the survey shows, this is not true. Both were consistently reported as effective sources when selectively utilized. In addition, they were found to produce effective leads.
- *It's not worthwhile to send resumes to employers other than for advertised positions.* This is poor word-of-mouth advice. Sending resumes to employers can be effective if directed to a specific individual (hiring manager recommended) on a selective basis. Combined with appropriate research to match the company's interest and needs to the job hunter's skills and experience, the resume can create positive attention.
- *Send your resume to the human resources or employment department.* Whether human resources or employment is an effective contact depends upon the circumstances. The *Job Hunter Surveys* show that the employment department is least effective as a contact source and human resources ranked fourth out of six sources evaluated by job hunters. However, when an openly listed, advertised, or word-of-mouth position becomes available, the human resources department should be worked along with the hiring manager. Your results will be greatly determined by how well you zero in on available jobs as shown by the *Surveys*. Remember, in some companies hiring managers have the human resources department or a designee do most of the screening. A good basic rule is to always attempt to contact or send your resume to the hiring manager or a designee, or a member of senior management, preferably someone related to your areas of skills and experience. You can always follow up with a contact to human resources.
- *Unsolicited resumes are not effective.* True and not true. The survey results point out that the effectiveness of unsolicited resumes is marginal. Both surveys provide suggestions to improve effectiveness. (See Chapters 3 and 10.) Selective matching of skill and experience to company and job improves effectiveness substantially. Unsolicited resumes can be effective and provide solid results where good skills or experience matching company needs is communicated. This is particularly so with cover letters and resumes directed to target companies developed by inquiry and introductory calls. Remember the advantages mentioned in sending them to the hiring

manager or senior management as cited in the *Job Hunter Surveys*.

In today's job market, a job search requires creative and assertive efforts. Everything should be tried and then judged by what works best for you. Take all your blinders off and pursue every avenue possible, particularly the effective sources the surveys indicate and that are suggested here. Studies show at least 70 percent of all job openings are not visible to job seekers using conventional job hunting techniques.

Bill utilized a creative technique in his job search. His friend Mary worked for a public relations firm and knew how to get articles placed in strategic media. He asked her to write an article about the latest computer innovations and include his program ideas for the future. Three major computer corporations got in touch with Bill through the public relations firm Mary worked for. He was offered consultant work by one company and a full-time position by one of the other two companies. Bill accepted the full-time position and was able to do the consulting work on the side.

The Major Sources of Job Opportunities

Effective sources for and avenues to job opportunities are extensive. In this section, I will review the major job source areas and avenues—visible/openly available, behind-the-scenes, hidden, and potential. To understand the employer aspect of job sources, I begin with the major sources of job opportunities, then move into discussing both traditional and nontraditional job sources and contacts.

The development of a job opening differs from company to company depending upon size, urgency, nature of the business, company policy, whether a human resources department exists, and whether a hiring manager is involved. In some companies, the process simply involves a hiring manager doing all recruiting and hiring. In others, it can be almost as brief. In still others, it can be a more formal and sometimes involved process. The eight-step process outlined in Exhibit A will help you visualize the entire process from the thinking stage to the highly active recruitment stage.

In reviewing the job opening and recruitment process keep in mind that this can vary from company to company depending upon size, culture, and flexibility. The outline in Exhibit A (see page 107) is a guide. The action column describes the formal action taken by the employer, and the status column describes the formal listing of availability of the opening by the company. Remember, informal action can occur in any of the stages. These actions do not necessarily conform or formally reflect what is stated in the formal action or status column. Therefore, actual activity may be different at times from what is formally happening when you contact the employer. This is a good reason not to take no for an answer on the availability of a job opportunity or possible opportunity when you are told by anyone other than the hiring manager that no position is available.

A search may be conducted in stages 3 through 8. In stages 3 through 5, a search is most often confidential. In some companies, a nonconfidential search may be conducted in any one of stages 4 through 8.

Understanding the process employers go through in creating a job opening and filling it will help you utilize the employer hiring process to your advantage. In some instances the human resources department may not know of a specific job opening until stage 4, and sometimes not until stage 5, which is one of the best reasons for job hunters to contact hiring managers.

The first six stages are ripe and rewarding job opportunity areas for the job hunter who goes beyond the limited traditional job hunting techniques. Many people limit themselves to traditional job hiring avenues within a company (stages 7 and 8). Numerous jobs are found in the first four stages by assertive job hunters willing to work and dig for these potential areas of opportunity. The initial stages are the behind-the-scenes job possibilities that offer a great opportunity to the assertive job hunter. This is because there are few, if any, candidates with whom to compete. The lack of competition in the job development stage affords an excellent opportunity to strike it rich before the hoard of candidates begins funneling through the company recruiting channels in the active job-availability stages. There are instances in many organizations where the personnel department will not know of a job search, often even for key positions, during these early stages; the exception might be a very astute human resources staff. However, if your resume and/or talent should show up and be presented at the right time and place, the job opportunity could well occur (as has often happened).

Many job seekers ignore these opportunities and sell themselves short in the process. This is the reason it is very important to follow up with employers when they do not have positions available. Then, if something does develop, you'll be one of the first to get a shot at the opportunity involved.

There are various reasons why "no opening" may be the reply to your initial inquiry. The following are typical reasons a position may never formally develop beyond stage 4 or 5: A confidential search; hiring manager knows an individual is suitable and quickly fills the position; an employee referral; an external prospect may develop or a reorganization or restructuring provides an internal prospect. Additionally, an assertive job hunter who discovers an opportunity in the behind-the-scenes or hidden job market may fill the position before it is known to be available. Keep in mind that a position can be in the development stages for many weeks. In some cases, positions have been known to lurk beneath the surface for months before a decision is reached or any formal action is taken.

Take a careful look at each of the eight stages of job development and you will discover opportunities you may have been missing. As an example, during stages 4 to 6, you still have an opportunity to beat the mass of resumes that flows into a company through their normal channels. For stage 5, a position may be open for weeks before action is taken to recruit for the position. In fact, the personnel department may still not even know the position is available. Not until stage 6, and most often stage 7, do conventional job hunters know about the opportunity.

At this stage, competition is often fierce and your probability of success drops measurably. In today's competitive job market many jobs are never advertised and never reach stages 7 and 8. Many developing jobs don't get beyond stage 5, and some jobs today are being filled in the first four stages. What all this means to the aware job hunter is that considerations for a job opportunity can occur long before a formal position openly exists. In an employers' market, assertive job hunters can make their talents known in the earlier phases of the job opening development process, and thus leave no stone unturned in finding opportunities.

Job Opportunity Sources

As you develop your job search plan, divide your sources into (at least) the following five areas:

1. Traditional job opportunities
2. Nontraditional/behind-the-scenes job opportunities
3. Hidden job opportunities
4. Job opportunities that can be developed
5. Target companies applicable to your skills and experience

Finding Jobs with Traditional and Nontraditional Job Search Methods

Traditional Search Methods

The following job sources should be included in your job plan. They should be reviewed on a regular basis.

Openly Available Sources and Avenues

- Sending resumes to companies
- Advertised positions
- Company open houses
- Data banks/networks
- Professional associations
- Job fairs
- College placement
- Search companies
- Outplacement firms
- State employment service
- Networking
- Posted positions
- Employee referrals
- Newsletters
- Trade associations
- Computer data banks
- Employment agencies
- Recruitment firms
- Nonprofit job groups
- Job clubs

Networking Contacts

- Search firms
- Company acquaintances
- Business associates
- Former employers
- Former work associates
- Hobby/club associates
- Professional/technical associations
- Social clubs
- Business clubs
- Civic groups
- Educational associates
- Sporting groups
- Training/industry groups
- Attorneys
- Insurance agents
- Product/trade groups
- Industry association groups
- Investment advisors
- Friends
- CPA firms
- Professional associates
- College alumni
- Church members
- Fraternity/sorority
- Relatives
- Vendors
- Service clubs
- Neighbors
- Volunteer groups
- Consultants
- Political contacts
- Business owners
- Financial associates
- Market research firms
- Bankers
- Advertising contacts

I have found, from the *Job Hunter Survey* results along with my personal experience, that many people go about their job hunting in a traditional manner, using only the openly available sources. Many job hunters fail to fully utilize all the networking contacts listed and fail to develop an effective systematic networking plan. Only a limited number of job hunters effectively use behind-the-scenes nontraditional sources. Some job hunters use target company search methods effectively, but the majority do not make good use of this technique. Even fewer job hunters use assertive inquiry call techniques to develop job opportunities. Traditional job hunting methods above can be effective in a good job market. In a tight job market, however, they can be limited and restrictive if not combined with the nontraditional techniques described below and include PEG matching. (PEG matching is explained in Chapter 9.)

Nontraditional Search Methods

To fully maximize your potential to find the ideal job, let's explore nontraditional job hunting methods, techniques, and sources.
These include:

- Behind-the-scenes job market opportunities
- Hidden job market opportunities
- New and unknown contacts (including those found by making cold calls)
- Working traditional sources with nontraditional techniques— assertive target company contacts, inquiry/introductory calls
- Sources developed by personal interaction/meetings (elbow-rubbing, personal introductions, etc.)
- Job opportunities developed through self-employment, entrepreneurial efforts, joint ventures, network marketing, and distributorships (These are discussed in Chapter 14.)

Take note that the last three are different forms of networking than the general networking utilized by many job hunters with friends, associates, and colleagues.

Jobs in the development stage of the job opening and recruitment process (behind-the-scenes jobs, including openings not yet approved) provide an excellent source for job hunters. When you add these openings to requisitions that have not yet been posted, advertised, or actually recruited for, the total opportunities on tap are enormous in relation to the number of jobs openly available. In a lean job market the number of positions in this category and in the not-actively-recruited category always increase. The large availability of candidates creates less need to recruit. It has been estimated that well over 50 percent of the jobs "in process" are in this category. This is because in the early stages of developing a position, employers generally take no overt action to fill it. Many positions are found in these early stages by assertive job hunters willing to search for these potential areas of opportunity.

Hidden Job Opportunities

Another category of job openings is purposely kept confidential by the powers that be. These jobs are in the hidden job market area. This term gives the connotation of keeping a job out of sight or secret. Clearly, the vast majority of jobs do not fall into this category, which often involves confidential needs. However, a fair number of executive and senior management positions occur in the hidden job market either through an internal or external executive search effort. Employers generally do not want their jobs to be known as hidden. However, certain available positions are hidden for confidential reasons, and those of you with a talent for private investigation will find some of them! These job openings can be described as internal or external confidential searches known only to the hiring manager and perhaps key personnel staff.

If you explore the behind-the-scenes and hidden job market in addition to traditional channels, you will at least double your potential job opportunities. Remember—you can develop job opportunities and be interviewed for potential jobs or jobs that don't formally exist. I have seen many individuals interviewed and hired long before the jobs formally existed.

Hot Job Possibilities Not Openly Available

Job possibilities can be in limbo for many reasons. The following are reasons a position may not be openly available and may never formally develop beyond the early stages:

- Pending discharge of employee
- Pending transfer of employee
- Co-worker or manager knows employee is looking for job
- Reorganization and/or restructuring of company

- Confidential product development activity
- Pending, revised, or new confidential marketing/business development effort and/or R&D effort

In all of the above situations, if you asked an employer if there were any job openings, the probable answer would be no. Traditional job hunters are bound to miss out on some of the better jobs, leaving them for the more industrious who develop strong employer source contacts and assertively follow up on them.

When Jake decided to move his family from Chicago to Florida, he told a friend from his college days who was looking for a job in the same field at the same level, that his job would be available soon. Jake's friend gave him a resume, and when Jake gave his resignation to his boss he also gave him his friend's resume. If you can find a similar situation, you can cut out a lot of competition!

Direct Contact with Company Management

Unleash your job search efforts by actively pursuing the behind-the-scenes job market. Go directly to company management and broaden your networking avenues as much as possible within a company's organizational structure. The following additional nontraditional job-hunting methods and sources will help you maximize your opportunities.

Developing New/Unknown Networking Contacts

- Develop contacts with companies who appear to have potential opportunities or needs for your skill and talent using inquiry and introduction calls particularly to obtain names of potential hiring managers.
- Contact unknown individuals (company and networking list based on possible mutual areas of interest such as business/ professional/technical and consulting interest; sports, career, association, college, etc.) All you need is an initial icebreaker to get the conversation going to gain interest. Contacts can be gained from your research and sourcing.
- Elbow-rub with managers and professionals in your job interest area whom you meet while attending meetings and other gatherings. Take the opportunity to gain introductions and develop rapport with these individuals.

- Assertively work all placement industry sources including search and contingency firms for leads.

These forms of networking are different from the networking you do with friends, associates, and colleagues. This form of networking is designed for targeting specific individuals and groups in your areas of job interest and needs. These contacts should be developed as if they were a market for a new product . . . you! Your list of known contacts will help as you begin to build your list of unknown networking contacts. There are many leads here. Don't hesitate to ask for them.

Target Companies

The purpose of developing a target company list is to provide you with potential employers suitable to your skills, interest, experience, and capabilities. In developing this list, be sure you first identify what specific areas of business and industry, by job area, you want to pursue. Chapter 6 helps you identify your areas of interest aligned with your skills, experience, background, traits, and so on. Then try to determine the employer's job need in your area of skills on an employer's need scale (high need, moderate, minimum, no need, or unique skill/one-of-a-kind need). The minimum need and no-need categories should not preclude you from working the company for behind-the-scenes or other potential opportunities. Keep in mind that companies are not always interested in making jobs openly available when they will receive a flood of resumes.

After you have targeted companies and organizations in your areas of interest you are ready to start your detailed sourcing (see source directories next page).

Job Sources—All Roads Lead to Job Possibilities

Contacts and meetings with both traditional and nontraditional sources are essential for most individuals, particularly in a lean job market. Be careful not to over-edit your contact list, as you may be editing out your best referral. If you must be confidential in your search because you presently hold a job, be extremely careful in your contacts. If you have any serious doubts about confidentiality, eliminate dealing with a questionable contact.

Source Directories

Many sources of information are available including those listed below by category. Additional major sources are listed in the Appendix, and an extensive list is available in the separate workbook. Contact the hiring managers or department, division, or general managers of those companies in your areas of interest.

- Business directories
- National directories
- Local directories
- NTPA (National Trade and Professional Associations)
- Chamber of Commerce directories
- Corporate reports
- Government directories
- Placement industry directories

After you have targeted companies and organizations in your areas of interest from your research and these directories or listings, obtain the name and phone number of the appropriate person to contact along with each company's full address. Now you're ready to start the ball rolling with directories and sources.

What Is Going on in the World?

Part of your search plan should include studying what's going on in the world. If you don't know, you can't carry on an intelligent conversation with your contacts and those who interview you. Whether or not you have a job, you are a vital part of the world, and you must continue to take an interest in it. Read business, industrial, trade, and financial journals, along with newspapers and magazines. Let employers know that you're on top of all the issues. This will give them the impression that you can handle *their* issues.

Job Search Plan at Work

Work the job market using the Job Search Plan Outline that follows. Work all avenues of opportunity, both traditional and nontraditional, and remember that adversity creates opportunity!

Job Search Plan Summary Outline

1. Get organized.
2. Clearly identify your skills, experience, training, and talent.
3. Determine your job and career interests, goals, and objectives.
4. Become knowledgeable about the job market.
5. Match your skills, experience, and talents to job market need.
6. Develop and execute your own tailored job search and marketing plan to gain employer interest and interviews—and offers!
7. Assess and access the job market for both available jobs and opportunities. Work all sources and avenues (behind-the-scenes, hidden, target, developed, and so on).
8. Be conversant on and knowledgeable about what is happening in your profession, career field, and related fields. Most importantly know what is going on in business and in the world today.
9. Polish all your skills (communication, presentation, and job) to meet job market need and stay ahead of your competition. Develop your presentation before you contact prospective employers and enhance it as your search proceeds.
10. Evaluate and recalibrate your search activities for effectiveness (matching job market need and results) as your search proceeds.
11. Continually use the new job search guides—*99 Minute Formula*, VWP, PEG matching, TNT, and TART. (See Chapters 4 and 9.)

SURVEY SUGGESTIONS

From Hiring Managers

- Have a good track record.
- Research the hiring company.
- Find and nourish mentors.

From Job Hunters

- Utilize 200 top executive recruiters.
- Hang on to your current job while looking.
- Set obtainable short-term goals in your search plan.

9

Marketing and Selling Yourself

Job hunters must assertively market and sell themselves to gain maximum job market exposure, both in developing opportunities and in taking advantage of existing opportunities. If you don't take advantage of these opportunities, believe me, someone else will! To market yourself successfully, you must research all possible job opportunities. (See Chapter 8.) To sell yourself, you must position your experience and abilities above that of your competition. (See Chapter 5.)

Meeting and Matching an Employer's Needs

The essential ingredients for job search success are:

- Finding a job opening
- Responding to a need or specific job requirement; developing an opportunity
- Matching your skills to the employer's need and gaining interest (retraining/recareering if necessary)

- Giving a successful presentation of your skills and abilities to a potential employer
- Attracting, negotiating, and closing the job offer

Adjusting and responding to the realities of the mid-1990s job market is essential in all of these areas, as shown by today's market conditions (Chapters 1 and 2) and the *Surveys* (Chapter 3). Job hunters succeed in today's lean job market if they can find and effectively respond to prospective employers' needs, have suitable skills and abilities to match, and make an excellent presentation.

Selling Yourself in Today's Different Job Market

The boom years from the mid-1970s through the 1980s were easy ones for job hunters who often had little competition and the pick of several job offers to choose from when changing jobs. During the years prior to the 1990–91 recession, employers developed all types of methods and plans to attract potential applicants, including offering a bonus for referrals, an up-front bonus, or a relocation bonus.

Today, the job hunter's easy-pickings job market has disappeared, and it will not reappear for years to come. Instead, we have an *employer's market* where jobs, particularly the better jobs, are often difficult to locate. Daily headlines since the recession tell the story over and over again: layoffs, reductions, early retirements, and plant closures. These often involve thousands of individuals per company. Few of the *Fortune* 500 companies remain untouched, and many small to mid-size companies are joining the downsizing phenomenon.

Let's look at one such situation and see how having up-to-date essential skills paid off for an individual laid off by a major company.

John Smith worked for CBS for over 26 years. They laid him off just months before he was to retire. What they didn't realize was that he was the only person who knew *all* the intricacies of running their teleprompter. When Dan Rather covers world or national events, he very often requests John. Hence, John is now working intermittently for CBS freelance because his essential skills keep him in demand.

If you have any doubt about the difficulty of today's job market, let me remind you of the *Employer Survey* response in which 86.5 percent of the respondents indicated they would reinstate less than 25 percent of their eliminated positions when the economy improves. In recessions prior to 1990, this figure was in the range of 60–80 percent.

The *Job Hunter Survey* provides ample evidence of the difficulty job hunters are having in finding jobs today. The survey data in Chapter 3 shows:

- The average time to find a job is 6.24 months, up since the 1990–91 recession.
- Almost 90 percent of job hunters reported their job search was more difficult than expected.
- Almost 90 percent spent more time than anticipated on their job search.
- The average number of contacts reported to obtain an interview was 24; for a job offer, 121 contacts.

My experience and the *Job Hunter Survey* does, however, show that job hunters who aggressively work the job market will succeed by:

- Developing job opportunities including the behind-the-scenes and hidden job market.
- Upgrading job skills/recareering.
- Discriminately responding to job opportunities and potential job opportunities with well-prepared research/sourcing.
- Discriminately matching skills and experience to employer needs.
- Utilizing effective presentation tools designed for today's job market (i.e., new job hunting guides presented, etc.).

When job hunters are willing to extend themselves with such solid homework and presentation efforts, combined with the broader approaches suggested here, they get results. Job hunters who improve the use of past traditional techniques and combine them with non-traditional and new avenues, techniques, and approaches, consistently report greater success in their job searches.

Experience in dealing with successful job hunters and the *Job Hunter Survey* shows which approaches are working more effectively today. Most of the success of these approaches depends upon self-generated job hunting efforts requiring a great deal more effort and time than past methods.

As you review the following effective methods of marketing and selling and the guides for job hunting success, remember that hours of hard work and an open mind are required for these methods to work. Your successful job search will involve a marriage of the *99 Minute Formula* and the New Guides described later in this chapter.

Effective Methods of Marketing and Selling Yourself

- Direct contact with employers via introduction and inquiry calls, letters, resumes, and third parties
  - Responding to known opportunities: Ads, postings, word of mouth, job fairs, employee referrals, open houses, job bank listings, and so on
- Developing and responding to potential areas of employer need
  - Technology developments, product/market expansion, organizational changes and new product development
  - Special needs and temporary requirements created by reorganizations and downsizing
- Developing and working target company list
- Job placement industry contacts
  - Executive search companies
  - Contingency search companies
  - Employment agencies
  - Job/data bank services
  - State employment department services
  - College placement offices
- Related placement services and activities
  - Volunteer groups
  - Job clubs
  - Outplacement organizations
  - Association referral assistance/services
  - Support groups
- Third party contacts
  - Networking
  - Friends
  - Associates
  - Associations, organizations, and groups (business, professional, community, volunteer, social, alumni, fraternal)
- Working the behind-the-scenes and hidden job market
- Developing cold contacts into live opportunities
  - Research and sourcing potential employers and hiring managers
    - Areas of known employer interest
    - Areas of potential employer interest
  - Inquiry/introductory calls to employers and related leads

- Temporary employment offering potential permanent employment opportunities
  - Temporary employment
  - Contract employment
  - Consulting
- Meeting with managers and lead sources in business, industry, and related areas (associations, seminars, professional/community groups) in areas of your job interest
- Pursuing recareering avenues, particularly in emerging industries
- Pursuing self-employment and entrepreneuring avenues

In today's highly competitive job market, you must communicate your skills, experience, and talents effectively via three methods:

1. Verbal, all of your spoken presentation (telephone, interview, follow-up)
2. Written: resumes and cover letter
3. Personal presentation

Moreover, you must communicate in a creditable manner that lets you stand out. Today, a person is seldom fortunate enough to find a job that does not require the standard American business custom of submitting a resume and completing an initial screening session. In an employers' job market where you are faced with lots of competition, be prepared for employers to evaluate your entire presentation effort—resume, letters, phone conversations, and interviews—including highlighting your past accomplishments along with what you can be expected to contribute in the future.

The *Hiring Manager* and *Employer Surveys* provide a key tip to job hunters on the all important aspect of presentation skills.

Let's look again at this subject and the survey response:

Question: What type of candidate shortcomings do you observe most often in today's job market?

	Hiring Manager Survey	*Employer Survey*
Answer:	Poor communication skills; poor presentation skills	Poor communication skills; poor presentation skills

Time and time again in my 30 years experience of working with job hunters I have found presentation skills to be the nemesis of many qualified individuals. This has become more apparent as we progress through the mid-1990s with a continuing lean job market. Job hunters often shy away from the critical self-evaluation this area requires. Often, job hunters struggle with this simply because they do not pay enough attention to the importance of making a better presentation. It is also an area where little preparation is done and minimal practice occurs.

The marketing and sales techniques recommended here are adapted for today's employer needs (based on my years of experience) and substantiated by responses from the *Surveys*. Most important to recognize today is the drastic change that has occurred in the employment environment and in hiring practices. Employers have much smaller personnel and employment staffs, which have many more candidates to screen and select from in much less time than in prior years. Much the same is true for hiring managers, who have assumed more duties, often doubling their responsibilities. As a result, it's harder to get a job. The following five new guides I have developed will help you be today's successful job hunter.

New Guides for Job-Hunting Success

Guide	Application
99 Minute Formula	Gaining employer interest: successful interviewing, attracting, negotiating, and closing the offer
Presentation (VWP) (Verbal, Written, Personal)	Your presentation to employer: resume, letters, interviewing
Matching (PEG) (Position Employer Guide)	Meeting/matching yourself to position/employer requirements
Traditional, Nontraditional (TNT)	Using nontraditional approaches combined with traditional approaches
TurnAround (TART) (Turnaround Retry, Turnaround Retrain)	Turning around rejection/no response to recovery and success

These five guides are tools developed for today's changed job market. The first four guides essentially involve the basic factors you deal with in your contact with employers. They serve as a guide for the job hunter's progression through the employer's selection process and help you understand how to deal effectively with employers. They include:

- Research/sourcing
- The resume
- The cover letter
- Job search techniques, sources and avenues to employers
- Initial phone discussions
- The initial interview
- The interview, attracting and closing an offer

Also included is the all important job matching process, which is essential for the successful job hunter.

If you follow these guides, you will find they help you stand out from the job-hunting crowd, particularly in your verbal, written, and personal presentations, which I refer to as the VWP presentation factor.

The Matching Guide involves the matching or pegging of your skills to today's employer needs (PEG-position/employer guide). The nontraditional guide (TNT) stresses using nontraditional approaches as well as traditional job search strategies and approaches. The Turnaround Guide is a recovery process for individuals who find it difficult or impossible to find a job that matches their skills. The Turnaround Guide (TART) is discussed in Chapter 14. In addition, Chapter 14 reviews a range of issues and techniques for struggling job hunters, including skills assessment, skills improvement, and new skill development to meet and match job market or potential employer needs.

You have now reached the step in your job search where your focus turns heavily outward. Marketing and selling yourself to potential employers in the best manner possible increases the likelihood of receiving a favorable employer response and an interview. Remember, if you don't stand out from the job hunter crowd, and you do a poor job of matching your skills to employer needs, you will be lost in the shuffle of hundreds of resumes and many phone calls.

I see job hunters consistently miss out on many opportunities through lack of knowledge and inadequate preparation and presentation. For example, the *Employer Survey* shows employers take an average of 30 seconds (or less) to screen a resume. Yet the large majority of job hunters today still use two- and three-page resumes that take a great deal more time than 30 seconds to read.

Many do not include a cover letter of introduction. Many of these candidates do not get results. If you want to be really effective in the initial presentation of your resume, it should be one page, well organized, easily read, and convey the message of your relevant qualifications and skills quickly, clearly, and succinctly. To get results, forget lengthy resume and lengthy cover letters. They rarely get read. The written presentation section (see Chapter 10) provides some new guidelines for your resume and cover letter presentation efforts.

The *99 Minute Formula* is key to job hunters in today's highly competitive job market. It says you have:

- 30 seconds to get your message across with your resume and cover letter
- 5 minutes to sell yourself on the telephone in an initial introduction or following resume interest
- approximately 1 hour to sell yourself in the initial interview
- 24 minutes research time to learn about the prospective employer

In total, you have a time frame of approximately one hour during which an employer initially judges your capabilities. Your initial employer exposure, if it depends upon a resume, involves a message that you must cover in 30 seconds.

This is a big task. If done right, it will result in positive employer responses. Since so much is at stake in the 30-second resume review period, you will find great emphasis placed on resume preparation in the upcoming resume and cover letter section. You will also find a separate section for:

- Employer telephone discussions
- Interviewing
- Nonresume introductions, where job seekers are urged to pursue initial introductory approaches other than the resume (Such introductions provide a better environment with greater time and a more appropriate setting in which to sell yourself.)

Keeping the new guides firmly in mind, let's review the key items involved in marketing and selling yourself to potential employers in the best manner possible.

Keys to a Successful Job Search

- Marketing and Selling Yourself: Do It

    It's critical. It's essential. And the power to do it is within your own hands. If you do not assertively market and sell yourself you will lose out on many opportunities that will go to other job seekers who do. If you don't "do it," who else will? Don't depend on others and wishes for luck to find the ideal job. Develop your search and marketing plan with a timetable for implementation and execution.

- Meeting/Matching Employer Needs

    Responding to an employer's needs in an appropriate fashion will greatly determine your job search success. (This includes having excellent presentation (VWP) and matching (PEG) skills plus developing further skills to meet employer needs, if necessary.)

- Homework, Investigation, Making Contacts

    Research, sourcing, networking, and elbow-rubbing are critical ingredients in learning about potential employers and prospective employers with whom you will interview.

- Best Possible Presentation

    Meet and match your skills to an employer's needs and then use extensive personal contact, letters, resume, telephone calls, interviews, and other methods to the best of your ability.

Follow All the Steps

Obtaining a new job for yourself today is a marketing and sales feat unto itself. The initial job search activities you have learned in earlier chapters have prepared you to enter this phase of your job search effort well armed with the tools for job search success. Getting familiar with the *99 Minute Formula,* beginning your investigation and research, and getting to know yourself set you on a successful course of action. These, combined with the marketing and selling skills you learn to apply, should lead you to the ideal job. If you skipped earlier chapters out of anxiety to get started on your job search, I suggest you go back and read them. They form the basic foundation for a solid job search effort.

Before getting into the total presentation aspects of your job search, let's quickly review some rudimentary steps in the employment selection process. These steps open your eyes to the tremendous importance your personal contact efforts play in a successful job search. There are generally six to ten presentation/communication steps a job hunter has with an employer in which to strike gold and get the offer or strike out and get the boot. Therefore, it is not surprising that employers in the *Survey* indicated presentation and communication skills are two of the most common shortcomings in today's candidates.

If you can picture the employer contact steps a job seeker goes through to successfully obtain a job, it becomes much easier to be a successful job hunter. Let's review these steps before you move on to the most important phase of your job search plan—presenting yourself.

Job Hunter Presentation Steps in the Selection Process

- Telephone call
- Resume/cover letter or letter
- Personal introduction
- Third-party introduction
- Interview
- Follow-up interview(s) (optional use by employer)
- Miscellaneous contact (optional testing, references, additional selection techniques)
- Follow-up contact (letter)
- Follow-up contact (telephone call)
- Closure

Note the number of times you have an opportunity to communicate with an employer about your capabilities, skills, and experience—and the number of times an employer has to evaluate and screen you for their decision. Now take particular note of the following seven criteria employers generally judge candidates by in their presentation.

Key Employer Candidate Presentation and Evaluation Factors

- Presentation
   Verbal
   Written
   Personal presentation: nonverbal as well as verbal
- Work history/experience and stability (verbal and written)
- Skills and ability (verbal and written)

- Education and training (verbal and written)
- Accomplishments (verbal and written)
- Related job activities and interest (verbal and written)
- Company/organization suitability (verbal)

Your Presentation: Verbal, Written and Personal (VWP)

To obtain an interview and then be selected as the final candidate who receives an offer, you have to meet the specific needs and requirements of a future employer. There are general requirements, qualifications, and skills you must meet in order to obtain the first interview. Most often, there are additional requirements, skills, and employer guidelines that you must meet to succeed in the interview as well as proceed further in the selection process.

In all aspects of the employer selection process, your ability to present yourself (VWP factor) in the best manner possible becomes one of your most important job-hunting assets. With some companies it may be the most important aspect of their selection criteria.

Your presentation tools for job search success depend on your ability to package and present your:

- Background (work history)
- Experience
- Education and training
- Skills and abilities
- Accomplishments
- Related interests and activities

The Presentation Guide: VWP

To simplify the presentation guide, all items relating to your verbal, written, and personal presentation activities will hereafter be referred to as your VWP. You want to be the person with the best VWP level possible.

Remember, in today's job market you must stand above the crowd. In past years there was no crowd with whom to compete and therefore little driving force to sharpen VWP skills. While VWP will not get you a job if you do not possess the basic skill qualifications or training required, it will certainly be weighed as a key selection criteria in your favor. If your VWP is excellent or better than that of a competitive candidate who has a relatively equal or close level of qualifications, you will probably be the candidate to receive the offer. I have seen many good candidates who failed to make the initial selection cut and the employer's final panel because they were weak in presentation efforts even though they possessed the skill and experience required.

You may now be asking yourself: Should I more carefully evaluate my own personal level of VWP skills? For many, the answer should be a most emphatic yes.

VWP Skills to Evaluate and Judge

- Verbal skills (telephone and interview)
- Written skills (resume and letters)
- Personal presentation skills (nonverbal, demeanor, attitude, dress, neatness, social, manners, and so on, see Chapter 11, your personal interview presentation)

If you are not satisfied with your skills in these areas, seek additional training and guidance. Various sources are available, such as outplacement consultants, job placement sources, counselors, Forty Plus (see Chapter 14), job assistance/self-help groups, and association placement groups. Be careful with the sources used, inquire about their qualifications, skill, and experience level; beware of retail job assistance firms who charge high fees.

The Matching Guide (PEG)

Matching or pegging your skill and experience to the position and employer you are interviewing with is a good common sense tool in the mid-1990s lean job market.

> The *Employer Survey* responses emphasize the need for job hunters to match background and skills to a particular position and the employer involved. The single most consistent recommendation by employers regarding resumes was that job hunters should cite relevant experience that is on target for the position or that matches employer requirements.

From the survey and my experience, I have coined an applicable acronym to help job hunters remember the important process of matching their experience to the position and employer, thus the position (P) employer (E) guide (G) or PEG.

Year after year I have listened to employers complain of the tremendous number of candidates who fail to match their skills to employer needs (PEG match) and thus are spinning their wheels. Simply stated, you want to put a round peg (your experience and skills) into a round hole (an employer's need) for a good job and employee fit. This will substantially improve your job search efforts and success. Solid skills and experience are essential, but you must also know how to effectively package and present them and work to match them with employer needs in order to gain employer interest. Job hunters who try to force a square peg into a round hole are working in the misplaced hope that the employer will hold onto their resumes. This process is often called "indiscriminate resume broadcasting" and provides few results.

The Traditional vs. Nontraditional (TNT) Guide

It is beneficial today for job hunters to be nontraditional as well as traditional in their approach to employers. Making inquiry calls to employers for networking, for identifying hiring managers, and gaining information are nontraditional approaches for many individuals. Incidentally, inquiry, introduction, and information calls are used extensively in the job placement industry.

The one-page resume presentation recommended in Chapter 10 and PEG matching are other nontraditional approaches developed for today's lean job market. *Survey* responses show that the use of lengthy resumes and long cover letters no longer meets employers' changing needs.

Be nontraditional, and do not hesitate to assert yourself by asking questions that will provide you with basic information about the job and company early in your campaign. In doing so, you can mentally prepare and structure your response to provide more meaningful data for matching your skills and experience to employer needs. The five-minute question-and-answer period in the *99 Minute Formula* is strategically located early in the interview in order for you to gain beneficial information for better interview performance and to serve as a natural transition after the chitchat stage during which you build rapport. This interview structuring will allow you to get to the pertinent job qualification areas quickly so that you can identify and astutely answer the important questions and address the concerns that arise.

Often when job hunters tell me they are bogged down in their search efforts, I ask them if they have put any real dynamite (TNT) into their search. It is very easy to fall victim to the traditional job search methods that worked for the 30 years prior to 1990. Today, nontraditional approaches (see Chapter 8) abound and are working. When combined with effective traditional methods, your job search efforts can be substantially improved.

The Turnaround/Retrain (TART) Guide

The turnaround/retry, turnaround/retrain guide is for the struggling job hunter to use for recovery in today's lean job market. When a job search produces few or no results, that is, if no offers come in after a reasonable effort, it's time to stop and take stock. Turn around and get back on track. It's time to analyze what has happened with your activity to date. It may also be the time for a major midcourse redirection and turnaround. You may find you need to try one of two approaches:

- Turnaround/Retry—with more effective effort and approaches
- Turnaround/Retrain—to develop new skills for today's job market need

To more effectively move your search forward, including recareering if necessary, utilize the *99 Minute Formula,* the VWP Guide, the Matching PEG, and the suggestions and strategies for problems and special situations provided in Chapter 14.

SURVEY SUGGESTIONS

From Hiring Managers
- Keep current with the job market.
- Learn about your prospective employer's business.
- Develop transferable skills.

From Job Hunters
- Keep trying . . . don't let the bastards get you down.
- Get a grip on who you are and what you want.
- Network, let people know you're looking.

10

Your Personal Employer Introduction

For the job hunter, all roads to a new employer lead through a telephone call, resume and cover letter, personal introduction, or third party. Job offers occur only after an effective introduction and winning interview. The importance of the introduction cannot be emphasized enough. Consider the fact that over 90 percent of all interviews occur as the result of a resume or telephone introduction.

The following presentation methods are those most often used by job hunters.

Gaining Employer Interest with Your Presentation

Type	Method
Written	The resume, cover letter and follow-up letter, application form, electronic communication, fax, E-mail, data banks
Spoken	Telephone calls, personal introduction or presentation, verbal and nonverbal forms of communication
Personal and third-party	Friends, business associates, employee referral, network contact, placement industry professional, and others—ultimately utilizing the material you present to them (spoken and written)

Experience shows, and the surveys confirm, that a variety of employer introduction methods (target mail, direct response to a specific employer opening or need, third-party presentation, introductory or inquiry call) are effective when used with (1) good homework, preparation, careful planning, and networking; (2) an excellent verbal, written, and personal presentation; and (3) tailoring skills and experience to employer needs.

Your Written Presentation

The resume serves as an indicator of you, your talents, and abilities. It is one of the more standard methods of introduction for executive, management, and professional job hunters. It is considered by many to be the most important written document presented by a job candidate. As we proceed to review effective resume presentation, keep in mind the cover letter that goes with your resume. The cover letter focuses the reader on the highlights of your career (skills and experience) and builds the reader's interest in your resume. In today's competitive job market, the cover letter is as important as the resume. I have found that many individuals do not take sufficient time to properly prepare either of these documents.

The Resume

> The resume represents 100 percent of what you are and appear to be, without your being present at the initial introduction. A poorly presented resume is the kiss of death. It will shut the door for an interview before you ever have a chance to get your foot inside to say hello—no matter how impressive your qualifications may be.

This is why it is important to read Chapter 6 on self-assessment. That is where you will learn about the tools necessary to evaluate yourself so you can to write an effective resume.

Here's an example. Joe had a very difficult time arranging his resume to fit on one page. He had been a vice president of finance and marketing, and he needed to convey a number of important strengths, including his ability to create computer programs, such as product analysis and customer evaluation, for various departments.

After using a three-page resume without any response, Joe changed his approach. He solved his problem by selecting a small but easy to read typeface and eliminating all but the essential elements of his last 15 years of experience. He summarized his prior experience in one short paragraph and dropped all detailed descriptions (providing only a brief overview) of responsibility and all school information, except degree and college. He also revised his cover letter to include a personal referral introductory note and directed it to a specific individual.

After sending out 30 resumes to hiring managers, he received 13 replies, 4 interviews, and 1 offer. This was a very good renewed (TART Guide) job search effort for the type of job market he had been experiencing.

Keep in mind the following comments I have heard from hiring managers:

- "If you could see the incredible number of poorly organized, prepared, and written resumes I have received, you would realize the negative impact they create."
- "I have seen many qualified individuals lose out on job opportunities because of resumes that were not brief, succinct (clear and concise), easy to read, and related to the employer's requirements. Many contain glaring errors, too many pages, a poor writing style, and/or a format that is difficult to read and follow."
- "A poorly prepared resume can cause a job hunter to lose more job opportunities than you can imagine in your wildest dreams!"

The Resume for Today's Job Market

The best resume today uses a one-page quick-glance reverse chronological presentation with a half to three-quarter page cover letter (see samples available in Workbook).

In my judgment, to make an excellent first impression, there are very few ways better than the one-page resume with a well-planned and written cover letter. This format allows the reader to pick out the highlights of your background and experience in about 30 seconds. Remember, you only need to gain initial interest. If you feel you have more background and detail that cannot be reduced to one page, you can provide additional information on a second page (two-page standard resume) or with an addendum to the first page. If you must have a second page, make sure all important data and your last 15 years of experience are on the first page. Further information should be reserved for the interview.

If you are having trouble reducing your resume to one page, I suggest you seek help from various sources such as outplacement specialists, human resources trained professionals (employment preferred), and from search-firm professionals and associates. These individuals can give you an objective overview and analysis that will be helpful. If you still find you are struggling with too much material, list additional items of accomplishment along with earlier job history on the second page. In establishing quick-glance interest you may entice an employer to browse your second page. Do not go beyond a two-page resume, and do not submit attachments. They simply are not read. Photographs are also a no-no. (Exceptions include jobs in the creative, design, graphics, and art areas.)

Let's look at the comments on resumes from the *Employer Survey* respondents as a guide for resume preparation and presentation. The *Survey* results about resumes summarize what, in my experience, shows most employers prefer today.

Resume Comments and Suggestions from EMPLOYER SURVEY (1993)

Type of Resume Preferred

Resume Format
   Chronological (89.74 percent preferred.)

Resume Length
   One page (72.94 percent preferred.)
   Two page (acceptable by 54.24 percent.)
   Over two pages (80.2 percent responded negatively.)

Resume Content
   Clear statement of job objective
   Work history (dates/places of employment)
   Job titles/brief job responsibilities
   Qualifications and experience
   Skills and accomplishments
   Education

Resume Features That Have Positive Impact

- brief
- clear
- concise
- easily read
- neat

- indicates expertise
- indicates stability
- accurate/factual
- uses bullets
- clean

- organized
- includes summary
- well-formatted
- well-written, good grammar
- matches experience to employer requirements
- states objectives

- no job gaps
- lists job titles
- uses highlighting
- can quickly see
- uses key words related to employer need
- up-to-date

Resume Features that Make the Greatest Negative Impression

- too lengthy
- spelling errors
- typos
- sloppy
- poorly organized
- no job dates
- poor quality
- grammar errors
- picture enclosed
- indicates poor stability
- too much information
- lack of focus

- narrative form
- lack of objective
- lack of clarity
- poor format
- unrelated experience
- job gaps
- unorthodox style
- handwritten
- poor copying
- canned appearance
- lacks information
- multiple attachments

Additional Comments

To make a positive impression, the overwhelming employer preference was for resumes that cite relevant experience and background, particularly when it is on target for the position sought and/or matches experience to employer requirements. Narrative resumes consistently received negative comments (60.3 percent). Letter-only queries without resumes received strong negative comments (84.1 percent). Cover letters were consistently requested. Specific employment dates and job history rank as the two most important items to include. Insistence on brevity was nearly unanimous.

The *Employer Survey* results also indicate that while unconventional resumes (cutesy, artsy, unusual forms, and so on) may get attention, they may not always receive the attention sought. This, however, should not discourage those involved in creative, art, or design positions, where such resumes may be useful and effective in demonstrating your talent.

In writing your resume, make sure you relate your experience relevant to the key qualification requirements of the position you are applying for. (A word processor or computer is essential for doing this efficiently, see Chapter 5.) Most importantly, in writing your cover letter, cite your experience to the top key qualification requirements and be sure they relate to your resume.

Years of experience and our research show most positions have a minimum of four to six key requirements. If you find the key requirements of the position are not clearly defined by the employer, draw them out in your preinterview discussions.

Cover Letter

> The cover letter submitted with a resume is one of the most effective tools a job hunter can use when it properly highlights the message you are communicating with your resume, particularly when it cites relevant experience and is addressed to a specific individual.

Essentially, you want to show your suitability to the employer's organization, requirements, and needs. The cover letter establishes a quick focus for the employer and, when well done, allows you to stand head and shoulders above the job-hunting crowd. It is a most effective method of communication in the following approaches to the employer:

- Cold introduction
- Communication following an initial phone call
- Third-party introduction
- Follow-up to personal introduction
- Response to advertising and openly available positions

It does not take the place of the personal introduction, which is ideal.

The importance of the cover letter was stressed in the *Employer Survey* where respondent answers to the question, "How might a candidate increase the effectiveness of resume contact?" were as follows:

- Include a cover letter
- Address it to a specific individual
- Follow-up by phone

With good investigative research and information-gathering phone calls, you can direct the cover letter to a specific individual. My own experience, along with that of various employers, indicates that this improves your chances of a positive employer response by at least 75 percent.

Application Blanks

The application blank is not an effective way to present yourself. For executives, management, and professionals, the application is not generally required in the initial phase of screening and interviewing. Use your resume whenever possible.

Some companies require an application blank be completed before an interview. However, many companies do not require an application until later in the selection process. For some trades, craft skills, and many nonskilled jobs, application blanks are often required. However, a well-prepared resume supplements the interview process and is a valuable timesaving tool in completing applications.

Read the application carefully, especially any agreement and stipulations section, and follow the directions explicitly. Remember, these forms are designed to fit an employer's specific needs and legal requirements. Complete the application as fully as possible. Where an answer is requested that is not applicable, write "Not applicable." Where an explanation is required, be brief. Make sure you are not providing any erroneous or inaccurate information or in any way falsifying application information. Be consistent with your resume when giving application data.

Follow-up Letters

A follow-up letter is an important tool in a job hunter's search efforts. It shows you have the courtesy to respond to an employer. It also serves as an accepted method of emphasizing what you have to offer and how the employer can benefit from your contributions.

A follow-up letter can be used after any introduction and should be used in any case where you feel there is a:

- Positive response
- Potential opportunity
- Need to thank someone who has provided a courtesy or information that was meant to be useful to you
- Need to provide additional data or to enhance your presentation

I recommend a follow-up letter after all initial interviews, whether a company expresses interest or not. You never know when a potential opportunity will occur and the follow-up letter may improve future interest and communication links. When interest is expressed, the after-interview follow-up letter is the time for a well-written, carefully crafted response, indicating interest and citing areas of mutual interest, benefits, and so on.

Your Verbal Presentation

Introductions, Telephone Calls, and Interviews

Your verbal presentation to employers involves your total introduction. It can include up to six forms of contact—or more:

- Introductory phone call
- Resume follow-up call
- Resume/letter follow-up requesting a call
- Personal introduction
- Interviews
- Follow-up calls

(Interviews and their follow-ups are covered in detail in Chapters 11, 12, and 13.) Keep in mind that verbal presentations involving nonverbal body language (physical movements, expressions, tone of voice) often have as much or more impact than what is said with words. Nonverbal communication is so important I have set aside a separate section in Chapter 11 to discuss its impact on the interview.

The Introductory Phone Call

The introductory phone call is your initial telephone introduction to a company. The introductory call occurs before you send a resume and is different from the resume follow-up call described in the following pages. This first call opens the door to many opportunities with an employer, with or without a resume, depending on a job hunter's approach. Its primary purpose is to gain an interview with an appropriate hiring party in your areas of skill, experience, and interest.

Remember, the introductory phone call can also serve the purpose of an inquiry, or can be used to set up a short informational meeting or a meeting to discuss potential consulting services. These, in turn, can lead to a job interview further down the line.

If possible, set up an informal meeting with the hiring manager. This is an excellent way to break the ice and make your best first impression by applying your presentation skills (VWP) and the techniques learned from the *99 Minute Formula.*

Properly planned and prepared for, the introductory phone call can help you learn of known job opportunities. It can also provide access to behind-the-scenes and hidden job opportunities. Your knowledge of the company will help you gain a positive response. It will show the individual you are calling that you are interested and have taken the time to learn about the company even though an immediate position may not be available.

The introductory phone call can also be your opportunity to present a brief verbal resume pitch. This is where the importance of knowing the what, where, when, and how of "XYZ Company" comes in.

In making an introductory or specific job inquiry call, you should be aware that some companies inadequately list or fail to indicate the key qualifications required for a job and make it difficult for the job hunter to obtain good basic job data. This happens less by design than as a result of developing brief job descriptions. Nevertheless, it can complicate the selection process for you and for the individual performing the screening and interviewing.

In medium- to larger-size companies, the detailed selection process is often delegated to the human resources organization. When only sketchy information is transferred between departments and to the interviewer or recruiter, a lack of clear understanding about the qualifications needed is sometimes created, and this can result in ineffective screening. This is another good reason for contact with a more appropriate individual in the hiring process, such as a hiring manager or staff member delegated by the hiring manager.

If you ask for a description of the job specifications and qualifications you can find out if they are known. It is important to both candidate and employer to understand what is required and what the expectations are for the individual being hired. This is what makes the matching process work.

One of the advantages in dealing with companies that are attentive to a careful selection process and have a quality human resources organization is that they are generally more knowledgeable and more responsive. This often makes it much easier for a job hunter to deal with the employer effectively.

Phone Call Objectives

- To introduce yourself
- To obtain information
- To present yourself briefly enough to gain interest
- To obtain an interview
- In lieu of interview, to send a resume to the appropriate hiring party
- To learn about the company—where you might fit in and fill a need
- To obtain information regarding:
    Specific positions available
    Pending opportunities
    Potential and future opportunities
- To develop interest where no available position exists

In reviewing the job opening and recruitment stages in Chapter 8, you can see that many potential job opportunities exist in the behind-the-scenes and hidden job market that you want to tap. Most important in your introductory calls is the possibility that you may develop an employer's interest, and this could lead to the development of a job or create action on a potential job that does not openly exist. A number of successful job hunters have told me of their success in finding a job through such contacts where jobs did not openly exist.

Let me give you a good example. I heard the following story from a company president with whom I had lunch. He told me he received a phone call from an individual he had met at a business gathering, whom he frankly could not remember. The individual indicated he would like to drop by for an 11:00 A.M. visit and a quick cup of coffee to see his facility. The visit turned into a lunch, and afterwards the individual said he felt he could be of help in several areas of the business. He wrote to the president with several of his ideas. A second meeting took place to discuss the ideas and resulted in a job offer and acceptance. Surprise! The candidate later indicated the introduction was planned, based on his research and sourcing. The individual's job search ended successfully when, after looking for many months, he instituted a nontraditional and assertive search effort.

The important item to remember here is that the introductory phone call initiated from various sources—homework, research, sourcing—and proved an effective method of opening doors to develop a job opportunity. In a competitive job market, do not hesitate to be assertive and use all approaches in making cold contacts and direct contacts with companies.

In all contacts with companies, make the contacts work for you. Should no immediate interest occur, determine the possibility of future interest, including a possible time frame. Ask for other potential job leads—it can't hurt!

Libraries, directories, data banks, and professional associations can provide plentiful leads for your introductory calls. In all cases, endeavor to obtain the name of a hiring party or line manager. Avoid those who are not in a direct hiring capacity.

Effective Employer Job Sources to Contact

The *Job Hunter Surveys* report which areas of an employer's organization job hunters find most responsive and effective:

- Senior management/corporate (43.8 percent)
- Line management (16.6 percent)
- Staff management (10 percent)
- Line management/corporate (6.2 percent)
- Human resources (5.5 percent)
- Staff management/corporate (3.5 percent)
- Staff/line (2.8 percent)
- Employment (1.7 percent)

My personal experience with job hunters has shown that it is more effective to contact hiring managers or other senior managers directly if possible. *If you are concerned about protocol,* you can always include the human resources or employment department in the loop. Remember, if at all possible, you want to use your best presentation effort to gain the attention of the hiring party, not of an intermediary.

Resume Follow-up Phone Call or Letter Requesting a Call

Generally when the employer makes a resume follow-up call or sends a letter requesting a call, it is for the purpose of setting an appropriate time for an interview. However, some follow-up calls are used as additional screening conversations. If you find the conversation is unduly long or involves a great deal of questioning on your background, don't hesitate to be assertive and suggest an interview date to cover the questions more thoroughly. Since your objective is to obtain an interview, provide essential but abbreviated information to gain it.

Using the Call to Prep for an Interview

To prepare for the interview, use the phone call to identify where the position is in the job development and recruiting process described in Chapter 8. Also ask what key qualifications the company is seeking in filling the position.

If you have responded to an ad, the ad will generally state some of the key qualifications. If the position is clearly identified and in the active recruiting phase, usually a position description has been written that defines the job duties, responsibilities, and qualifications desired. If the position is in the developmental phase, it may not yet be clearly defined. If the position is in the active recruiting process, you know you are going to have extensive competition for the position. If the job is in the open and not-active recruiting process, you will have less competition. If it is only in the development stage, you will have far less competition. Knowing what stage the opening is in will assist you in planning your approach and strategy for dealing with the company.

Regardless of where the position is in the job development and recruiting process, try to determine the key qualifications before the interview, if at all possible. Prior to your interview, request a copy of the position description. If one is unavailable, discuss the position briefly over the phone so that you can be informed. This can be handled effectively by advising the hiring manager or interviewer that you want to make sure your background is suitable and you don't want to waste their time. Most personnel interviewers and hiring managers will appreciate this approach. If it is not possible to obtain the key job qualification factors in advance—because they are still being developed, or the job is not in the active recruiting stage—then wait and inquire during the interview question-and-answer period. In some instances, discussions between a prospective applicant and employer will help the interviewer to clarify the specifications of the position.

Virginia, a director of data processing at a large company in Dallas, told me she ran up against a stone wall in her attempts to find out about job requirements before interviewing for her current position. As a last resort, Virginia took the initiative and called the company's vice president of data processing. The vice president was delighted to tell her not only all about the requirements of the job, but also the pros and cons of the job and about all the people in the department as well.

Virginia arrived at her interview thoroughly educated as to the position and the company culture. She received an offer, accepted it, and has been with the company for a little over one year.

First and foremost, try to determine if you are qualified and reasonably suited for the job in advance of your interview with the company. If you are not suitable for their immediate requirements, but feel you are potentially suitable to the company, it can definitely be worthwhile to pursue the contact. A "no job fit" introduction or any introduction that leads to other job opportunities is definitely worthwhile. This is particularly true if you have determined from your research that there is a reasonable probability your qualifications and skills may be of value to the company in the near future.

The Personal Introduction

Most personal introductions involve a third party and a social setting or business meeting setting of some type. In any case, the purpose is to gain sufficient interest to obtain an interview. The social or business meeting I refer to here involves what I personally call "rubbing elbows" with a potential hiring manager or a lead to a potential hiring manager. In such situations your initial introduction should be social with business kept to a minimum, unless it is understood to be a business meeting.

Third-Party Introductions

Third-party introductions are one of the most effective entries to employers and should be cultivated in your networking as much as possible. It is to your advantage to work with and through an individual who is in some way associated with or known by the company. The introduction, therefore, provides you an entree otherwise unavailable. Remember, a third-party introduction essentially evolves from what you do in your written, verbal, and personal presentation efforts prepared for the third party. Take some care to assure you are accurately represented and put in your best light by the third party. This means keeping tabs on the third-party sources being used, sources such as search firms, agencies, network sources, employee referrals, professional associates, and others. Historically, third-party introductions have been one of the most effective means of obtaining an interview. An effective third-party introduction creates a favorable condition for the job hunter because the introduction most often comes from a proven and known source considered worthwhile by the employer.

Success Story Using Inquiry Calls and PEG Matching

Let's look at an actual case. Ted Smith, a successful marketing manager with an electronics systems company, was looking for a job better suited to his growing management interests. Ted utilized many of the successful techniques presented here, particularly the PEG Matching and introductory-inquiry telephone techniques.

Ted was an assertive job hunter willing to take the time to develop opportunities in the early stages of the job development and recruiting process. He realized there was much less competition for these potential opportunities. From his mailings and calls to employers from his target list, Ted ferreted out a potential opportunity from a company matching his experience and background.

One of Ted's inquiry calls to a business associate helped him identify the potential job opportunity. He called the company personnel department, which was unaware of any opening, and followed up with a call to the hiring manager. He was then advised that the marketing manager was traveling, but his assistant mentioned a possible opportunity in the development stage and led Ted to believe it could already be in process. A follow-up call to the personnel department once again brought a "no opening" response.

Ted made several additional inquiry calls and discovered the position was indeed being formalized and struck gold in finding the job with a search firm that was just starting the search. Ted proceeded to gather data on the company, called the search firm for detailed information on the position, and asked for a copy of the job qualifications profile. He responded with an excellent one-page cover letter and one-page resume. They were tailored to the position, citing relevant experience that matched his background to the company need (PEG matching). He followed up with a phone call to the search firm to keep his name visible, endeavoring to maintain a high priority profile. The search firm received over 800 responses. Ted received an interest call within several weeks. During the interest call Ted gathered substantial additional information on the company, the position, its history, and particularly the type of person desired—beyond the basics of experience and education—in terms of culture, chemistry fit, special skills, and interest desired. As a result of a lengthy discussion of job responsibilities, challenges, and his own qualifications, Ted arranged an interview with the search consultant.

Armed with the results of good homework on the company (annual report, 10Q, market reputation, hiring manager profile) Ted made such a good impression at his interview that he was selected as one of three finalists. From questions Ted developed, he responded with a solid company interview presentation where he showed sound market knowledge and identified the company's two most pressing needs. As it turned out, those pressing needs (strategic planning and new product business development) matched his greatest strengths. Following a meeting with the company president where strategic planning was the focus of discussion, he was asked to provide a lengthy list of references. An offer followed within weeks. A counteroffer successfully concluded the exchange. Ted's job search story—from initial contact to negotiated offer, involving each step (approach, resume, letters, questions, etc.)—is recounted in the Job Search Workbook. (See last page of book.)

SURVEY SUGGESTIONS

From Hiring Managers

- Try many approaches.
- Be aggressive and take the initiative.
- Be flexible.

From Job Hunters

- If you fit a specific job description you have a chance.
- Networking is the name of the game.
- Set up a second source of income while looking.

11

Your Interview Presentation

The crucial minutes in the job search process come during the job interview. All of your job search efforts lead to this one important challenge. How well you do in the interview and how well you prepare for it determine whether you win or lose the job. The interview is the place where you take center stage to display your experience, skills, talents, and abilities in a performance that can make you a star.

According to the hiring managers surveyed, poor communication is the biggest failing of job candidates. A poor presentation takes second place among job candidates' failings. On the *Employer Survey*, poor communication and poor presentations came in number two and three as the biggest failings of job candidates. This up-to-the-minute information should tell you where to put your efforts!

The interview is often the job search step least well prepared for and practiced. Once on center stage, your preparation time has run out! There are no more trial runs, and the results are final. An excellent interview performance gains respect, recognition, and positive reaction. A poor performance often ends the show.

With communication and presentation playing such important roles in finding a job, some job hunters find it helpful to visualize the interview as a three-part process that requires rehearsal practice and a trial run before the actual show. This chapter deals with part 1: Your Interview Presentation, which includes your final preparation for the interview and your personal presentation. Chapter 12 deals with part 2: Interviewing Questions and Answers, the exchange between job hunter and interviewer, which is the heart of the interview process. Part 3: Successful Interviewing (Chapter 13) covers attracting, negotiating, and closing the offer.

Let's begin with a quick overview:

- Your interview objective: Obtain a job offer.
- How?

　　Follow the VWP Guide (Chapter 9).

　　Match your skills to an employer's need (PEG Matching, Chapter 9).

　　Know about interviewing (Chapter 10–12) and the employer selection procedure (Chapter 7).

　　Follow the *99 Minute Formula* (Chapter 4).

Learn to Work the Interview Process

From the employer's perspective, the main purpose of the interview is to gather information from which to judge your suitability for the position. This involves two-way communication with both verbal and nonverbal elements. The prospective employer's impressions and final determination will be influenced by your presentation, including verbal and nonverbal forms of expression.

Lydia always made an excellent presentation, both in writing and in person. She was a pro at dancing around questions she didn't like to answer. The interviewer asked her if she was proficient in Lotus. Lydia stated there was nothing speedier than a Lotus. She started talking about racing cars and switched back to computers with the statement, "Speaking of computers, I'm a real pro when it comes to Wordperfect, and by the way do you prefer working with an AST, Compaq, or IBM?"

Lydia was thoroughly qualified for the job, except she didn't know the Lotus program from Adam. She received the offer and began work. At the end of her first week, she was asked how she got the job without knowing Lotus. She said she told the interviewer she knew how to drive a Lotus, never that she knew the Lotus computer program. Her fellow workers had a good laugh and taught her Lotus.

Key Employer Interview Evaluation Factors

The various factors that reflect you as an individual during the interview are:

- What you say: your verbal presentation
- How you say it: your nonverbal presentation (your body language, involving facial expressions, body movements, posture, carriage, tone of voice, and eye contact)
- The outward impression you present
  Self-assurance and confidence
  Personal grooming, including dress and neatness
  Demeanor
  Attitude
  Ability to relate to others, involving congeniality, friendliness, and social skills
- Your skills, experience, accomplishments and capabilities—known as your "can do" job factors
- Your interest and motivation—known as your "will do" job factors. Also your work history and job stability
- Your education, training, and credentials
- Suitability to company culture and environment

Mastering the Interview

The interview itself generally involves seven steps and is conducted under five different formats. Procedures for interviews vary greatly because they reflect the skills and personality of the interviewer and the company culture. In most cases, a basic data-gathering session evolves from the following steps, not necessarily in the order indicated.

Interview Steps

1. Introduction
2. Brief "ice-breaking" period
3. Brief introductory statement from employer regarding the position and the company's needs
4. Employer questions regarding your experience, skills, abilities, and accomplishments; often additional questions about your background and interests, reason for leaving, and so on
5. General discussion, questions and answers, expressions of level of interest (More information may be provided about the company.)
6. Summary: A culmination of the continual matching process, beginning with the introduction, to ascertain your ability to meet the position requirements and company needs (Some

interviewers may express this suitability with a yes, no, or maybe, at the end of the interview, or they may need to continue the evaluation process in relation to other candidates or gain comments from others in the organization before providing a response.)

7. Closing options: an offer, pending decision, further review, additional interviews (2nd round), rejection, indication of consideration for other positions or future opportunities, hold on file

Types of Interview

The type of interview format may include any of the following. The first three are more common, with the group interview becoming more popular in the '90s due to the adoption of participative management styles.

1. *Directed Interview:* questions and answers that generally involve a one-on-one format of interviewer and candidate, with interviewer asking a variety of questions on key evaluation factors previously cited.

2. *Highly Structured Interview:* involves a more formally structured interview format that includes a lengthy list of questions asked of all applicants and generally is one-on-one.

3. *Nondirective Interview:* generally executed in a one-on-one format; the interviewer asks few questions but uses open-ended statements such as, "Tell me about your job, your career progress, accomplishments, and successes." A skillful nondirective interviewer will not overtly give the impression of covering most of the key employer evaluation factors and may actually cover more.

4. *Group Interview:* not extensively used, but becoming more common today; may involve several individuals from various departments, departmental managers, potential peers, subordinates, or employees. With the stressing of teamwork environments, more peer and subordinate involvement in the interview process is taking place in today's selection process.

5. *Stress Interview:* a format that can be done on a one-on-one or group basis. The interviewer(s) try to stress the candidate with questions. The objective is to assess the individual's reaction under stress and/or the pressure of a particular situation.

Successful Interviewing

The *99 Minute Formula* tells it like it is—how to prepare and present yourself successfully for the most important step in your job search: the interview. Let's begin your quest for a job offer with four fundamentals of successful interviewing:

1. Complete your research on the position, the employer, and the employer's market.
2. Prepare and practice your presentation.
3. Apply the New Guides described in Chapter 9.
   VWP Guide
   PEG Guide (matching skill/experience to need)
   99 Minute Formula
4. Be as up-to-date as possible on today's job market and the business world. Make sure you know about the company with which you are interviewing. It is much easier to carry on a conversation when you know something about the company (and the interviewer if possible) and are current on what is going on both locally and throughout the world.

Win or Lose in 99 Minutes

The interview is truly your chance to be a star. You have the opportunity to hit a winning home run or to strike out. Most "strikeouts" occur as the result of a lack of preparation, practice, training, and skill to match employer need—four basics for interviewing with success.

Interview Preparation

Begin the interview process with preparation. Preparation and the presentation that follows involve several important components:

- Introduction
    - Present an excellent first impression by being prepared with solid first impression techniques: appropriate dress, grooming, confidence, and friendliness.
    - Be alert and make a careful assessment of the interview surroundings and environment.
- Break the ice with chitchat to build rapport and common interest.
- Utilize discovery techniques in learning about the job and

company by completing inquiry, and information calls and good research.

Ask questions.

Utilize the answers in developing your presentation.

- Present your experience, skills, abilities, and accomplishments through your verbal and nonverbal communications.
- Actively participate in the interview (general discussion, mutual questions, expression of interest) and informally lead the interview if necessary.
- Understand the interviewing techniques used by many employers including additional third-party interviewers (boss' superior, peers, subordinates, work teams, etc.)
- Understand the optional screening techniques used by a few employers, such as trial-run presentations, sample work problems and sessions, a psychological summary or evaluation, testing, etc.
- Make a summary presentation (show skill to need fit).
- Close the interview with a positive clincher.
- Follow up.
- Negotiate. Improve, accept, or reject an offer.

Interview Preparation Checklist

Now that you know what to be prepared for in the interview, let's begin your preparation using the following 12-item checklist.

1. Prepare personal presentation.
2. Learn about the company.
3. Learn about the job.
4. Match your skills to employer needs with the matching PEG.
5. Note the questions you want answered.
6. Review how to handle interview questions.
7. Review the questions most often asked, including the tough ones.
8. Be aware of illegal questions.
9. Visualize your success by setting the stage and playing the role (practice).
10. Know yourself.
11. Avoid fear and anxiety by practicing the art of self-confidence.
12. Utilize some interviewing basics.

Item 1: Your Personal Interview Presentation

Your personal presentation is the image you create, involving the total picture you present during your interview. It begins with your introduction.

Your Introduction

Be friendly, smile, be positive and enthusiastic. Shake hands firmly and make sure you obtain the name of the interviewer and his or her relationship/position in the organization (ascertain in advance, if possible). Break the ice with friendly chitchat as quickly as possible. As you enter the room, assess the interviewing environment. Where are you expected to sit? Endeavor to select a chair next to the interviewer or at the side of the desk, if used. Try to avoid sitting with a barrier, such as a desk or conference table, between you and your interviewer. If you have the option, choose to sit on couches or chairs versus a desk; choose the former to create a more open and cordial atmosphere.

Observe your surroundings—the furniture, wall hangings, pictures, awards, plaques, and school and training diplomas. Also note magazines and professional, sport, or hobby items on the desk and tables. They indicate the interviewer's interests. These tips can spark good conversation and build rapport. Keep the atmosphere cordial, and note how the interviewer begins to structure the interview.

Build Rapport and Win the Job

Ken was applying for a position as quality manager. Aside from being accustomed to making an excellent presentation, he had learned to be very aware of the business environment. Ken noticed that the man who interviewed him was a Little League basketball coach. Ken was a soccer coach. They ended up having drinks after the interview to discuss coaching and their children's athletic abilities. This added rapport surely helped to make him one of three finalists for the position. In the last round of interviews with the president of the company, Ken noticed a rare plant he had on his desk. It turned out the president's hobby was caring for the many exotic plants and flowers he grew in his hothouse. After a little prompting from Ken, the president spent half the interview talking about his plants and—you guessed it—Ken got the job!

Get Organized

The following checklist will help you organize your verbal and non-verbal presentation:

- Personal presentation: chitchat
    Your introduction
- Your communication: verbal and nonverbal
    How you say it: your nonverbal presentation
    What you say: verbal presentation
    Learning to be a good listener and observer
    Your demeanor: social skills, manners
    Your attitude
    Your image and self-assurance
    Your personal grooming

Your Verbal and Nonverbal Communication

A successful outcome to your interview depends upon how you organize, package, and present yourself. It is important to visualize your total presentation. Be conscious of your body language, facial expressions, and gestures. Make sure they do not detract from your words. Studies have shown that in personal communications, such as an interview, the message received by the interviewer is judged heavily on both verbal and nonverbal communication.

> *Verbal Presentation:* your tone of voice and manner of speaking
> *Nonverbal Presentation:* your body language, facial expressions, posture, carriage, and gestures

In other words, you are judged on *what* you say as well as *how* you say it. The latter often can have as great an impact as the former. When facial expressions are combined with verbal communications, a total visual and auditory impression is formed.

Verbal Communication: What You Say

How well you speak and how confidently you state your case, are both part of the impression you will make on your interviewer. You will need to be organized in your verbal presentation. The 12-item checklist earlier in this chapter will help you prepare to present your thoughts clearly. Be cognizant of your voice inflections and if they reflect stress and anxiety. Be aware of your attitude. Speak clearly, with conviction, and at a good audio level, so the interviewer will not have to strain to hear what you have to say. Be careful not to speak in a weak, timid, or monotone voice.

On occasion, it can be useful to ask the interviewer questions about certain items in your presentation. These are in addition to questions you ask about the job and the company. You can ask if more information is wanted on a certain aspect of the responsibility you have described, a project or accomplishment you were involved in, or a thought you have expressed. Don't hesitate to convey confidence.

Study your annoying habits in order to avoid cliches, repetitive vocal and facial expressions (including excessive smiling), shifting in your chair, and so on. Never chew gum!

Keep your presentation clear, concise, and to the point. Don't ramble, particularly on items that appear to be of little interest to the interviewer. You will find it very helpful to outline your presentation in advance, to insure that you don't leave out any important items. A solid introduction and opening is essential to your presentation because the first four minutes often form a first impression that is difficult, if not impossible, to overcome.

Learn to be a Good Listener

Effective interviewing requires good two-way communication. This means both individuals listening carefully to what the other has to say. Be attentive to the interviewer. Listen carefully to the questions posed so that you clearly understand them. If you are not sure about a question or statement, ask for clarification or for the question to be repeated. A word of caution! Some job hunters become so involved in talking during an interview that they don't listen and don't respond to all the questions asked by the interviewer. Be careful about talking excessively and not listening and watching for the interviewer's reaction.

Learn to be a Good Observer

As the interviewer observes the job hunter's demeanor, so should the job hunter observe the interviewer's demeanor. In addition to our earlier comments about observing the company's environment and the interviewer's office environment, observe the interviewer's tone of voice and particularly the body language. This can be a tip-off to the interviewer's feelings about how the interview is progressing.

The more interviewing you complete, the more observant you will become.

Social Skills and Manners

Your behavior has substantial impact upon other people. If you present yourself (whether personally, on the telephone, or in writing) in a proper, professional manner, you will be judged accordingly. Good social skills require that you know the socially correct way of behaving. If you feel your social skills leave something to be desired, purchase a copy of an etiquette book (Emily Post's or Amy Vanderbilt's). This will serve as a useful source of reference for a lifetime.

Attitude

An important consideration in any interview is the attitude conveyed by the job hunter. Many employers judge heavily on attitude and that includes your basic attitude about work, your fellow employees, superiors, and current or past employers. Make sure your attitude is positive—a "can do" attitude gets the job done. Show you are a contributor, a builder who can be an asset and add value to the job, the team, and the company.

An astute interviewer will immediately recognize a negative tendency on the part of the job hunter. If for any reason a concern should develop about your attitude, run a reality check on it immediately. Negative attitudes can be an instant turn-off, and sometimes they can develop without a job hunter knowing it. The cause can be length of time on the job market, continued rejection, a poor experience with a former employer, or having been laid off or cutback. Even if these are temporary negative feelings, make sure they do not surface in an interview. Business associates, superiors, former superiors, family members, and friends may be helpful in running an attitude reality check. Most often a third party who does not know you, such as an outplacement counselor, will be the most help. This is because friends and close associates tend to shy away from offering critical suggestions.

Personal Grooming

Immaculate grooming and conservative dress are a must. Clothing should be neatly pressed and color coordinated, as well as appropriate for skin tone and hair color.

Always determine whether your attire is appropriate for the company and the position level. For a man, a suit with dress shirt and tie is appropriate for a formal business meeting. For a woman, a business suit with appropriate accessories should be worn to a formal business meeting. Informal dress may be appropriate in some companies, but is more often the exception than the rule for interviewing. It is best to check with someone you know at the company or someone that knows a lot about the company as to the accepted mode of dress. If all else fails, visit the company and see for yourself! In certain factory, shop, or similar work environments, wash-and-wear clothing is appropriate. If you don't have a flair for fashion, check the business or society section of your local newspaper to see what people on the level you wish to attain are wearing. Browse through news and fashion magazines, too. When you arrive at your interview, before you have had a chance to open your mouth, you will have already made your first impression with what you're wearing, with your grooming, and by your opening approach and nonverbal communication.

Several years ago, I interviewed a man for a position as director of engineering. He arrived from out of town in a sport shirt and slacks and wore white socks. Fashion at its worst! I told him, if he was interested, to come back after lunch wearing a dress shirt and tie with dark-colored socks, and at that time I would interview him for the position. There was no way the company president would have given him more than a 30-minute courtesy interview dressed as he was. He came back properly dressed and eventually received an offer. The reason he got a second chance was because he offered a very difficult-to-find talent.

SURVEY SUGGESTIONS

From Hiring Managers

- Maintain a sense of humor.
- Speak clearly and confidently.
- Never burn your bridges.

From Job Hunters

- Network continuously.
- Work like a demon.
- Highlight your strengths.

12

Interviewing: Handling
Questions and Getting Answers

Most individuals involved in a job search today, particularly those involved in substantial interviewing, will have either sensed or experienced tougher or more demanding employer job requirements. Certainly my experience shows such change and, in fact, dramatic change on the part of some companies. As pointed out in Chapter 3, the *Surveys* clearly show these changes, including those in the selection process involving candidate shortcomings and sought-after skills. The extent you will experience these changes depends upon your involvement and success in interviewing and the ultimate end results, that is, whether you receive an offer, a rejection, or learn that no suitable opening exists.

Completing the Interview Preparation Checklist

In the preceding chapter, we covered initial interviewing basics involving the 12-item interview preparation checklist, your personal presentation (item 1 on the checklist), and verbal and nonverbal communication. Here we continue with items 2 through 12. In Chapter 13 we conclude the discussion with a look at attracting and closing the job offer.

Item 2: Questions about the Company

What do you know about the company, its products, markets, people, organization, and culture? Who do you know at the company, or who can provide you with information on the company and the job? Who do you know that might have a lead in the company for you to contact? Inquire if the company is having problems to determine how you can apply your skills and experience to their need. If there is a specific job available or job areas of interest, what can you find out about the hiring or department manager involved and what problems may exist that you can help solve?

An annual report, 10K or 10Q report, and other company publications will provide very useful data. Specific industry and industry association publications, plus *Dunn & Bradstreet Reference Book of Corporate Management, Standard & Poor's Register of Corporations, Directors and Executives,* and other business related directories will also provide good data. Market industry reports, product data, and publicity releases will also give you viable information, particularly if the company in question is not publicly listed.

It is generally not difficult to obtain a copy of the company's annual report and other appropriate company publications, such as quarterly reports and newsletters. All of this literature will help you obtain a good overview of the company.

Item 3: Questions about the Job

What do you know about the job, its requirements, and how it matches and relates to you? Are there similar jobs in the industry where you can get information? Ask business associates, company suppliers, and customers. The best source is to call the company or a competitive company to get data on the job or a similar job. In addition, some associations and compensation consulting firms maintain job description data. Various industry and related association reports are also available.

Item 4: Matching Yourself to Position and Employer (PEG)

How do you match up with the company, its organization, culture, structure, and the job? Do you believe you fit into the company, its make-up, structure, and style? (See Chapter 9 for PEG matching.) The important consideration in PEG matching is to zero in on the company's needs and match your experience to those needs as closely as possible. For an existing opening, if an employer does not feel a good match exists, you will not gain interest. For other openings or future interests and needs, you may gain an employer's interest, based on solid matching of your skills to other areas where an immediate need may not exist but future ones may occur. My experience in recent years has consistently shown that employers endeavor to find the perfect match when filling a position. They want what I call the walk-on-water (WOW) candidate.

This is the direct result of the economic law of supply and demand. Employers are responding to the large surplus pool of talent available and being more demanding and more selective. Both the *Hiring Manager* and *Employer Surveys* confirm the trend of employers becoming more selective in the hiring process. In addition, a 1994 American Management Association survey of employers highlights this job market condition.[1] In that survey, employer responses showed that 28 percent indicated competitive pressures forced them to find a "perfect match" when filling a position.

In search assignments I recently completed, employers told me they would only hire an individual who met the maximum hiring criteria established. Interesting to note in these searches is that the new hiring criteria established involves a broader range and more demanding qualifications than previously required for the same position. Further, some employers have indicated they are willing to wait until the "perfect match" is found and, in most cases, this match can be found by waiting a few weeks or several months longer. Many times you can be a "perfect match" or a close match, but your resume doesn't reflect it because it was written for the masses.

Tom wrote an individual cover letter and tailored specific aspects of his resume for every company on his target list so that he could match his experience, skills, and talent as closely as possible to each company. With a computer and some reasonable knowledge of a word processing program, Tom found the matching process much less difficult than during a previous search he'd done before he developed his computer skills. While the initial target list work took some time in the beginning, he found a new job in much less than the average 6.24 months. As a matter of fact, he ended up with two

---

1. "Many New Executives Being Discharged With Stunning Speed, Statistics from Recent American Management Report." *Wall Street Journal,* 4 April 1994.

offers, the first coming five weeks after he mailed out his resumes and the one he accepted nine weeks later.

With the extensive competition for jobs in recent years, it is obvious that employers are going to pick the best available talent and respond to those who match their skills and experience to employer need.

> Remember, for decades it had been difficult for employers to pick the "cream of the crop" or WOW candidates. Now they can. This trend, along with lean operating management, will need to run its cycle before it reverses itself.

The important question for job hunters is: When will the job market reverse course and become more favorable to a job hunter? Will a job hunter's market return in 1996 or not until the early 21st century? In the meantime, job hunters should be aware of the necessity to PEG match their skills and experience to employer needs in order to gain interest.

Item 5: Questions to Ask the Employer

In my 40 years of experience in dealing with the job market, job hunters have consistently stated they wanted more information on the company in the initial interview. It is interesting to note that many employers have also commented that candidates have not, as a rule, asked many well thought-out questions. If we are talking about an initial interview, it may be that the job hunter was not given adequate information from which to formulate questions. This information may be given to job hunters in subsequent interviews. However, if the job hunter has researched the company properly before the initial interview, at least some good questions can be developed from this information, as the *99 Minute Formula* suggests. It is generally to everyone's benefit to clearly understand what the job entails and requires. This basic information should be provided to the job hunter, who in turn should provide the employer with a clear picture of his or her capabilities and interests.

I encourage job hunters to obtain as much information about the job qualifications and requirements as possible without being aggressive to the point that employer interest is discouraged. Use discretion in formulating your questions. Save any ticklish questions to ask until after you have built a good rapport with the interviewer. Initially, endeavor to obtain basic information regarding the job qualifications. Ask questions about the company's history and performance as the interview progresses. Be aware that it is difficult to determine how a company may respond to some questions, particularly if they misinterpret your motive for asking the question. If you are in doubt about how a question may be received, hold your question until serious interest is expressed or you receive an offer from the company. Some financial and operations questions about the company might not be answered until an offer is made. Be prepared, in some cases, for certain financial information to remain undisclosed or unavailable until you are employed. Even then it may not become available for some time to come. It is important for job hunters, especially for senior-level positions, to conduct a "due diligence" inquiry to obtain as much information as possible before deciding to accept a position. Don't hesitate to ask questions of knowledgeable individuals not currently associated with the company. A list of key questions to ask employers is provided in the Appendix. A lengthier list is available in the workbook.

Item 6: How to Handle Interview Questions

Be prepared! Gather information on the company and the job in advance. If possible, ascertain how your background and experience is suitable before the interview begins. This can be accomplished through the match-up process that you should complete when you either:

- Select the company
    As a target company for your job search list
    By responding to an available opening or ad
    By approaching the company for a specific reason

- Ask basic questions about the job or company in your
    Introductory call
    Resume follow-up call
    Interview

Don't hesitate to inquire about the qualifications required prior to the interview. Do your best to evaluate the suitability of your background, experience, and skills for the position and general needs of the company.

Utilize the *99 Minute Formula*—the question-and-answer period—to ask questions about the job and the company. At this point, you should begin to obtain some feel for the position and the qualifications involved.

During the question-and-answer period, it is most important that you begin to show the knowledge you have gained from your research on the company, its business, products, and marketplace. This will provide you with a tremendous advantage over candidates who are uninformed. Imagine the advantage you offer if you are applying for a job in the sales organization and you are knowledgeable about the company market, its products, and the competition, particularly with a product area in which the company may be struggling and has just made plans to introduce major market changes. I have seen many candidates vault to the head of the company selection list with good research completed and questions asked before the interview.

Questions Employers Ask

Questions come in several categories, but most generally relate to:

- "Can do"
- "Will do"
- "Adaptive"
- "Expectation"
- "Suitability/Culture Fit"

"Can do" questions. These are basic questions about whether you can do the job. Such questions include your strengths and weaknesses and relate to basic areas such as:

- Skill and skill levels
- Years of experience/work history
- Education and training
- Special capabilities
- Accomplishments

"Will do" questions. These relate to whether you "will do" the job aside from whether you "can do" the job. In addition to the basics of the above five areas, be aware that the employer is also seeking information as to your "will do" capabilities to perform the job well in areas such as:

- Attitude
- Enthusiasm
- Interest
- Conscientiousness
- Motivation
- Dependability

"Adaptive" questions. These are asked to determine your adaptability characteristics in relation to the employer's work requirements and environment. They include areas such as:

- Flexibility
- Ability to relate to others
- Open-mindedness
- Ability to listen
- Willingness to learn
- Willingness to accept responsibility
- Work ethic

Listen carefully to the questions asked and try to ascertain whether the interviewer is directly asking a question related to specific areas of basic qualifications ("can do" factors) or to "will do," adaptive, or expectation factors.

Performance "Expectation" questions. These occur when an employer is seeking to evaluate the expected level of performance for the job vs. the candidate's actual level of performance, training, and capability. This type of question will also allow you to consider whether or not the company's expectations are realistic.

It is worth remembering that expectations are a dual-edged sword for both job hunter and employer. Expectations can differ from the world of realistic performance. Employers' expectations often center around their anticipation of gains (likely, probable, projected) or success achieved by the new hire. The gains are often aligned with the employer's estimated level of candidate performance, capability, and training vs. the current or previous employee performance level. I have seen some hiring managers jump to conclusions over a new hire's expected level of performance. This can occur when the candidate's capabilities are not carefully evaluated or are overestimated in a new job environment. Such results can lead to disappointment and sometimes rapid disenchantment of both parties, particularly the employer whose expectations have not been met.

"Suitability and Culture Fit" questions. These enable the company to ascertain whether you will fit into the company over the long run.

Many employers consider this area of questioning critical to the hiring process. This is because the answers will tell them whether you have the ability to work harmoniously within the framework of the organization and its culture, and with the various individuals within the organization.

You should also measure such suitability to make sure the company, its organization, its people, and the hiring manager are a suitable match for you.

General Rules for Answering Questions

Answer the questions with a reasonably brief response. Don't go into lengthy details. Put yourself in the best light possible. Should you feel the interviewer is seeking an answer to a question other than the direct question (hidden-agenda questions) or the interviewer has a concern not being addressed, ask for clarification. If necessary, respond with several questions yourself to probe for the real questions or concerns. Be careful in this approach and sensitive to the interviewer's queries. Should the interviewer probe for further detail, be prepared to respond and don't hesitate to ask for further clarification if you need it.

Should questions occur that ask you to present confidential, proprietary, or unfavorable facts, data, or information, be cautious. There may be reasons, involving your own interest or your current or former employer's interest, that require you to withhold such information. If you are in doubt, say so and refrain from providing the information until you are sure you can do so. State your concern clearly when you refrain from answering a question. Indicate that you will double-check the advisability of providing the answer. In confidential areas that concern market, product, pricing, or financial performance data, confer with your former employer or seek legal counsel before answering such questions.

Close difficult interview questions in a straightforward and positive manner. Endeavor to shift to positive areas that put a favorable light on questions and take the focus away from negative areas. For instance, if you don't have the 15 years experience as a manager in one job desired by the employer, focus on the 9 years experience you have in three different jobs with two companies—all involving the latest modern management techniques. Keep the interview moving on to other aspects of the positive contributions you can make and other important qualification requirements.

As the interview progresses, take mental notes on what you feel are "hit-the-jackpot" questions. Also take mental note of the questions you feel you may not have answered as favorably as you would have liked.

As you approach the interview closing, ask how the interviewer perceives your qualifications suitability. Remember the interviewer's perception may well be different from yours. If you feel there are areas of concern, cover them again in your closing. You may or may not want to further probe these areas of concern, depending upon their extent and how well you can provide additional information without causing even more concern.

Always try to close any areas of concern. If you feel there are critical areas that may affect the interview's positive outcome, ask how such areas would affect the preferred profile of the person the employer desires to hire. In your closing, you can specifically address a major shortcoming in a positive light with questions and statements indicating your adaptability and willingness to learn.

Cynthia's story is interesting in this respect. Instead of having a problem with work skills or experience, Cynthia had a problem in getting along with people, particularly when divergent opinions were involved in working on some functional department issues. She was often impatient and narrow-minded when others' point of view differed from hers. To make things worse, she was outspoken. "Hopeless," you say. Well, not quite. In an interview for a job she was otherwise well qualified for, she admitted her problem and said that she was being counseled for it. In addition, she described a management course she was taking which delved into the best ways to get the most from employees, which included, of course, how employees should be treated. The company was so impressed with Cynthia's honesty, and her efforts to solve her problem, that they gave her the job on a probationary basis.

Item 7: Questions Often Asked of Candidates

Job hunters often ask me about questions that come up in the interview (more so after the interview occurs than before) that appear to be unique, unusual, or difficult to answer. Over the years I have kept track of some of these questions and found they vary greatly depending upon the nature of the industry or business involved and the individual's profession and level. It is apparent, though, that certain questions may be classified as troublesome depending upon the individual and the degree of difficulty concerning the subject.

A sample list of basic questions asked of candidates can be found in Appendix A. Some 30 questions are listed as a guide in six categories:

1. Employer/former employer
2. Job performance
3. Relating with others
4. Personal preference
5. Sink-or-swim questions
6. Schooling/education questions

An additional list of some 75 questions is available in the workbook. Be prepared to handle the basic standard and expected questions you are asked in each category. The more questions you review the more prompted you will be in the interview. Good preparation will help to cut down the percentage of questions you will find troublesome. Endeavor to develop your list so you will be sufficiently prepared to avoid being stumped. If you don't know the answer to a question, say something like, "Let me think about that," and arrange to get back to the interviewer with the answer.

I have categorized the questions listed in the Appendix by areas, which will ease assimilation and memory retention. This will also help in dealing with questions sequentially, as you review your background, work experience, education, and training. As you review the list, other questions may come to mind. Keep a list of these questions and add them to your database for practice and source material.

Item 8: Illegal and Troublesome Questions

Questions that relate to hiring decisions regarding age, religion, sexual orientation, national origins, and physical handicaps are illegal questions and are discussed in Chapter 14.

Troublesome questions are described as those more difficult to answer, perhaps because they hit an emotional nerve, relate to differences of opinion, revolve around performance issues, reasons for leaving, differences in philosophy, styles of management, or personality clashes. Regardless of what questions cause concern, reviewing questions, working them through, and developing a response, will greatly help in mastering successful interviewing. If you find certain questions push your hot button and create a response that could affect your presentation, work out positive answers.

Item 9: Set the Stage and Play the Role— Visualize

Visualize the interview and the various steps involved. Anticipate the questions and answers (yours and the employer's). Visualize how you will present yourself. Practice. Practice. Practice! Visualize success. Repeat this performance for each and every interview. Keep in mind the entire interview process, the New Guides, and other tools to work with, including the *99 Minute Formula,* VWP guide, and PEG.

Item 10: Know Yourself

To create an effective presentation you must know your skills, strengths, experience, and special capabilities inside and out. If you don't, no one else will! (This subject is dealt with extensively in Chapter 6.) These attributes form the foundation of your presentation. They are what you are all about. The presentation you make is your opportunity to package and present your skills and talents so you will stand out from the rest of the job-hunting crowd.

If you discover that your skills and experience are consistently not evaluated high enough to obtain interviews, reevaluate your skills and experience level for today's job market needs.

Should you discover, however, that it is your presentation efforts that are the problem, then you must immediately begin to rework your presentation, utilizing the new VWP, PEG matching, TNT, TART, and 99 minute formula guides. If it is not your presentation and you determine that you need to improve and update your skills, begin an assessment to determine what additional training is necessary. Review Chapter 6, and read Chapter 14 for further help.

Item 11: Self-Confidence—Avoiding Fear and Anxiety

Never, never go to an interview without preparation. One of the most important benefits of using the interview preparation checklist is the confidence you build to handle a successful interview.

The more you interview, the more comfortable the interview process becomes. Good research and preparation can help to minimize, if not substantially eliminate, stage fright. A certain degree of anxiety will help you keep alert and on your toes during the interview. Remember that interviewers are people just like you, and many are not trained in interviewing. Be prepared for a poorly trained interviewer. If the person is really inept, try to help him or her along with the process. You will both benefit. This type of situation can be to your advantage because you can steer the course of the interview according to the *99 Minute Formula*. Asking questions or clarifying information often helps to move the interview along. Asking open questions and getting the interviewer to talk about the job and the company provides you with data on needs, interests, and activities you can respond to.

Item 12: Utilizing Some Interviewing Basics

Interviews generally last for a limited time so don't do all the talking. Make sure you don't ramble on with answers and with nonrelated information. Careful listening is essential. The interview is a two-way form of communication, so it is important to avoid long-winded responses. Save time for the vital information you want to obtain about the job and the company. This information will help you determine whether or not you want to work for the company and the people involved and perform the job described to you.

If you find the interview is progressing satisfactorily and you are interested in the position, do not hesitate to ask questions about the goals you will be expected to achieve if you are chosen for the position. In asking certain questions, it may be wise to indicate that you want to judge the company expectations for the position in relation to yours, so that neither are tremendously unrealistic and no mismatch occurs. By being positive and taking the initiative, you deal in a positive way with a concern many employers have recently expressed and that also surfaced in the *Hiring Manager* and *Employer Surveys*. Should mutual interest develop, remember to ask in your closing remarks for a written description of the position and duties involved. If none is available or written, ask if one will be developed so you can review it together with the interviewer.

There are many reasons for reviewing the position description, duties, and responsibilities. Foremost is to make sure they are clear to everyone involved, that you understand them, and that you can determine what is expected of you. Secondly, what you see and are told is not always what you get! Discussions by all parties involved, particularly the hiring party, helps to clear any gray areas that may exist and reveal unwritten expectations or duties. Quite a few terminated or mutually resigned employees are haunted by expectations that never surfaced or were not made clear in the interview or upon hiring.

Sometimes job hunters complain that the interviewer did most of the talking. A one-way employer interview is okay as long as you get an offer. In such a case, you will want to make sure you are getting sufficient data to make an intelligent decision.

Above all, remember that your ability to concisely and credibly articulate your qualifications, to match your skills to employer needs, and to show that you can add value will be essential in obtaining the ideal job in a lean market.

SURVEY SUGGESTIONS

From Hiring Managers

- Improve your skills.
- Highlight your ability to manage people.
- Acquire new skills.

From Job Hunters

- Be flexible on money, location, and title.
- Join a professional networking group.
- Assess your future job career path.

13

Successful Interviewing: Attracting, Negotiating, and Closing the Job Offer

Y ou have to feel successful to be successful. And to feel successful, you must be confident in your abilities. If you have read Chapters 1 through 12 and followed the *99 Minute Formula,* you have begun to understand the job market and what's required in your journey to find the ideal job. You must know:

- The job search process, including effective sources for today's job market
- The employer selection process
- How to deal with today's changing job market

In addition, you must be willing to increase your job search efforts and continually upgrade your skills and credentials. Stiff competition requires that you stand out in the packaging of your skills and experience as well as in your verbal, written, and personal presentation.

Determination is a necessity! Don't take no for an answer, unless your competition has already accepted the offer. Don't fall for the standard "no interest" line or the "don't call us, we'll call you" scenario. Follow up on every possible job opening from every possible angle. Use your creativity in a professional manner to let prospective employers know you are the best person for the job. Be positive, assertive, and friendly as you communicate your qualifications and how perfectly they fit the requirements of the job. Avoid any display of negativity and never imply you are being ignored or misjudged, or that an employer has been remiss in any way. Concentrate on your qualifications and the contributions you can make to the company.

Years of experience in working with job hunters and recent survey responses support the following recommendations for attracting interest and achieving success:

1. Develop a sense of success. Stress confidence. Project a successful image. Maintain an enthusiastic attitude.
2. Be resourceful.
3. Develop and maintain a good track record.
4. Apply successful methods of communication, as stated in the *99 Minute Formula* and the VWP, PEG, TNT, and TART job guides. Make a continuous effort to achieve your goal—the ideal job.
5. Discover your talents, all of them, including those that are not apparent on the surface. Then apply them.
6. Gain positive response with a job search plan tailored to you, today's job market, and employers. If your search bogs down, analyze your shortcomings to determine the need for redirection or recareering options.
7. Success depends upon you, the methods, procedures, and the process you apply as well as your ability to deal and work with others effectively.
8. Be flexible, patient, and open-minded as you work all avenues, sources, and employers. Continually develop new job sources and follow up your networking efforts.
9. Attract interest with relevant questions, and be a careful listener. Ask yourself how employers and those with whom you network are reacting to you. Learn what attracts an employer's interest and is effective.
10. Be innovative and use nontraditional job search techniques along with traditional techniques that gain attention and response.
11. Know what's required in today's job market and apply your up-to-date knowledge to each job opportunity you discover.
12. The key to surviving in a difficult job market is knowing the market, working the market industriously including predicting where job growth will occur, and making sure you have the skills to step in and meet employer needs. Remember, the changing nature of the today's business world demands a new breed of job hunter, one who is flexible, responsible in

making sure his or her job skills training/development are up to date, inventive, assertive in seeking out and developing opportunities, and able to work with minimal supervision.

Convincing the Employer of Your Qualifications

The *99 Minute Formula,* outlined in Chapter 4, was developed sequentially to help job hunters present themselves in a convincing manner to prospective employers and in a format targeted to most employer selection processes. Review this formula often. It will help you successfully navigate the employer selection process. The first seven steps of the formula involve achieving success up to the critical phase of closing the interview. We will now go into detail about power-closing your interview.

The process of closing an interview should really start before the closing begins. That might surprise you. Your questions and discussions during the interview will have prepared you for an appropriate closing—a summation of why you are the best candidate for the job. Your prior research and inquiry calls to a company should allow you to communicate your suitability not only to the job but to the company as well. The many techniques used to gain information during the interview (asking questions, careful listening, probing for areas of preferred candidate strength, and so on) will help you close the interview by summarizing the superior advantages your experience offers in matching job and employer requirements. Note the following example.

In an assignment recently worked for a director of materials in a division of a major *Fortune* 500 corporation, three candidates presented excellent qualifications. Two of the candidates had previous experience in accounting and cost accounting. One of the candidates, Steve, learned through his inquiries, of a serious materials flow, inventory, late parts, and costing problem. He zeroed in on the uniqueness of his experience to show the substantial value he could add in solving an immediate and serious problem. Steve recognized, in addition, that the company had a strong financial orientation, and he showed his strengths appropriately. In fact, he worked the interview process to his benefit by suggesting a meeting with the division vice president of finance who was impressed with Steve's prior experience in accounting, cost accounting, and material monitoring systems. The deciding factor for Steve in receiving an offer was his familiarity with the vice president's special problems, which he had learned of through a mutual acquaintance.

In your closing strategy, the following questions can be asked to ascertain where and when you want to apply key statements to solidify your ideal qualifications suitability in the interviewer's mind:

1. How do you feel my strengths match the needs of the position and the company?
2. In what ways do you see my skills, background, and experience contributing to the job?
3. Are there any areas of concern to you in regard to my suitability for the job?

Ask the last question if you feel the company has concerns about your suitability for the job. After each interview, be sure to send a note to each individual who interviewed you. If you discover in the interview that a major shortcoming may exist, indicate that you are adaptable and willing to quickly learn what is necessary because you have a strong interest in the job and the company. Inquire what can be done to bridge the gap. Stress your willingness to complete any additional training on your own time and at your own expense. This approach has worked successfully for any number of individuals I have known. Most often, the key was the candidate's positive attitude, willingness, and other overall strengths, communicated in an excellent presentation.

I know of very few situations in which a candidate has been successful in overcoming major qualification shortfalls with an average presentation. A solid presentation is a necessity in almost every case in the current lean job market. All of the above questions give you the opportunity to respond affirmatively to any concern about your skills and experience in a positive manner before closing the interview. Endeavor to close the interview in a manner that avoids any lingering doubts that could be left hanging in the interviewer's evaluation. As you close the interview, make sure you offer a brief summary highlighting the contributions you can make to the company because of the solid match your experience makes to the company's requirements.

If you have a good feeling about the job, the company, and the match—in other words, there is a comfortable chemistry between you and the interviewer—don't hesitate to indicate how well you believe you fit into the organization and to show your strong interest in the company. If you are not interested in the job, don't string them along—word gets around—simply advise them in a positive manner and thank them for their time. If you're interested in the company but not the job, leave the door open for further opportunities by indicating your favorable impression and suitability for the company and its culture.

If the interview creates mutual interest and an offer is not immediately forthcoming, close by indicating you will call within a week to inquire whether they need further information. Indicate that you look forward to the next step in the selection procedure and to the opportunity of meeting again for further discussion. If the employer has indicated there are further steps in the selection process to complete before reaching a decision, you will probably have several follow-up phone discussions.

Some interview closings go on for too long. Interest can wane when this happens, so be prepared to move the process along by asking if there is any further information the interviewer would like. Measure the response by asking several questions that speak to the level of interest on the part of the company, and ask about the next step.

Determining the Next Step

If it has not been covered in the closing by the interviewer, it is appropriate to ask how the selection process will proceed. Attempt to determine when a final decision is anticipated and particularly what the next step will be (as it can be one of several). You can lead into the subject by offering references or providing additional information that may be appropriate.

Should you find that the employer does not openly offer information or much direction about the level of their interest, tactfully encourage clarification of their interest level. Interest status can often be obtained by indicating that you would like to contact the company in the coming week should any further questions arise. The employer's response to such questions will most often be a cue as to the level of interest. If an offer is not made during your interview, and there is no indication it will be forthcoming, it is important to begin building further interest through your follow-up efforts.

If the interviewer begins to close the session and there are still points that were not covered or clear to you, do not at this stage overpower your interviewer with a barrage of questions. Ask only a few of the most important questions, because persistent questioning may create a negative response. You can cover the balance of your questions in a subsequent discussion, follow-up phone call, or letter.

Interview Closing and Follow–Up

Interview Closing Procedures

Many hiring managers and personnel interviewers will close an interview by asking for a list of references or reconfirmation of certain data. Further expressions of interest can come in various forms such as:

- A request for additional background data to check—references, as well as education, degrees, and other credentials
- A second interview(s) with subordinates, peers, work teams, and additional superiors
- A request to complete an application blank
- Further selection procedure evaluations (testing, work example problems, a presentation session, a psychological appraisal)
- A tour or visit of the facility or additional facilities
- A visit to the local area for candidate and spouse, if they live outside the area

Follow-Up Procedures

I consider it essential to respond within 24 hours in writing with a thank you follow-up letter. Your letter should thank the interviewer for his or her interest and time, reiterate your interest in the position, and briefly highlight your suitability for the position, the contributions you can make to the company, and any other noteworthy comments. The letter should be one page or less, with good organization, good grammar, and absolutely no spelling errors or typo's.

How well you follow up, including your attention to references— or what I call indirectly orchestrating the follow-up process—is an important part of your presentation and can have considerable impact on the final decision process. It's a time when you can display your capabilities, leadership, poise, creativity, and thoughtfulness.

Should the interview not result in an offer for the specific position you interviewed for, more suitable opportunities may occur in the future. Good follow-up will provide the opportunity to inquire about other leads or sources from the interviewer or hiring manager. This is why it is so important to develop and maintain a good relationship with every prospective employer.

Follow-up Things to Do

- When applicable, communicate with hiring managers in an effective "provide and ask for information" exchange.
- Prepare your references and be ready to present them upon request.
- Contact your references when an employer indicates they will be checked.
- Perform a reality check on your interest and fit for the job and company on a long-term basis. Ask yourself if you can handle the responsibilities and if the job meets your objectives.

Receiving the Offer: What to Look for, What to Consider

Be pleased, positive, and enthusiastic, even when the offer does not meet your expectations. Keep a written record of the offer extended, as well as notes on the salary, total compensation, title, responsibilities, your potential working relationships, benefits, and so on. Ask for an offer confirmation letter. If no offer letter is provided, confirm the offer in writing to the party extending the offer. Defer your decision until you receive a written offer or until you confirm that the employer has received your letter confirming their offer. If the employer wants to discuss a potential starting date, it is appropriate to do so if it is in your best interest. Generally it is better to defer establishing a probable starting date until the offer is confirmed and you have had a chance to carefully review it. You must determine whether there are items you need to negotiate or evaluate against other offers, your job search activities, progress, and goals, before making a decision. Many items can be included in an offer. Always get the important items covered in writing.

The offer letter should include the basics of compensation (salary, bonus, incentive(s); start date; person, manager, or department you will report to; and, possibly, a brief description of your responsibilities (if not provided separately). Other important financial information to get in writing includes travel and relocation expense reimbursement, the benefits package, and any special employment terms (severance/termination if applicable, employment contract). Items not ordinarily covered in writing are covered in company policy manuals and benefits literature (employee benefits, health insurance, holidays, vacations). Request a copy of this information if you do not receive one. Don't jump the gun! Endeavor to determine the full extent of the responsibilities and duties of the position involved. Make sure you have obtained all the basic information necessary to make a sound decision—including such additional criteria as performance guidelines that involve bonus or performance plans, promotion potential, and a copy of any employment agreements and items you are asked to sign.

Analyzing and Negotiating the Offer

An aware job hunter should start preparing for potential offer negotiations before they occur. Preparation should begin during serious job discussions, at the time you learn about the company culture, history, and detailed requirements of the job. It is also helpful to learn if the position has been difficult to fill and how long the position has been available.

When it comes to compensation, set guidelines for yourself and then inquire about all salary and compensation items involved. Handle serious salary discussions with diplomacy, and get all compensation items out on the table. Just because a form of compensation has not been originally offered does not mean it cannot become part of the discussion and possible agreement. Strive to draw the employer out on the salary and compensation items being considered. Attempt to learn the total salary and compensation parameters involved for the position so that you can negotiate with intelligence. Determine when reviews and salary increases occur and if they come at the same time or at a different time. Learn about bonus and performance award payments and how, when, and who qualifies. Consider benefits as standard unless one or several are substantially better than the industry norm.

For many job hunters the most important item of concern will be compensation. For some it may be moving and relocation expenses, or deferred compensation or working conditions. For others it will involve one or more important items for consideration, such as growth, better immediate opportunity, more responsibility and challenge, better employer, better career track opportunity, or a more appealing work environment. Should you determine you want to negotiate, prioritize your list of proposed offer changes and negotiate the most workable issues first. Work toward a mutual agreement that results in a win-win situation for both you and the company. As you negotiate, make sure you have good reasons, such as proven ability to perform, in making your requests. Be realistic. When a deadlock occurs, suggest an alternative.

Sandy was over $15,000 short of the salary she wanted for the position of executive vice president of a New York retailer. She had the feeling the company was not going to budge, so she began thinking about what perks could take the place of the money. Sandy had longed to spend time with her young daughter and suggested spending one day a week working at home. She would communicate with the company via computer, FAX, electronic mail, or modem. She also requested a month off during the summer (the slowest time of the year for the retailer) in addition to the two week vacation they had offered her. To Sandy's delight, her alternative to a higher salary was accepted.

Evaluating the Offer

Don't rush into a decision, whether it be acceptance or rejection, until you have given yourself the opportunity to evaluate all aspects of the offer. The basic categories of items that can be included in a job offer are listed here:

- Salary
- Additional compensation
- Benefits
- Relocation and travel costs
- Special benefits and allowances
- Transportation/allowance for employee travel
- Expense reimbursement
- Charge card usage
- Special in-home reimbursement
- Additional

In considering an offer, be sure you analyze the company, its financial condition, stability, and viability. Always ask the company to provide a copy of its annual report and quarterly summaries. Additionally, ask the hiring manager and human resources department about the company's financial condition and profitability. If the business unit you are interviewing with is not broken out in the company's reports, be sure to ask about its condition and profitability. For private companies such information may not be available but may be provided in a different nonpublic format and often on a more confidential basis. Some private companies tend not to provide financial information until an offer is extended. The extent of your inquiry will generally depend upon the level of the position and responsibilities being considered. If the position is middle-level management, professional, or lower-level, a solid inquiry involving the company's profitability, business conditions, and growth projections, and a review of its annual report should provide appropriate data.

For senior positions, particularly those involving key management, financial, and P & L responsibilities, very careful evaluation and in-depth "due diligence" study is recommended.

Ask the company hiring manager and human resources if there are any particularly adverse known business conditions that would affect the viability of the company, the job, department, or business unit involved. (In other words, will the job be there in two years?) You want to gain as much information as possible. Gathering first-hand information is essential, although it may not always be accurate. Further checking with business associates, banking references, vendors, suppliers, customers, additional financial sources, and company financial reports should be done if any concern exists.

Techniques to Improve an Offer

I am consistently asked by job seekers who have received an offer whether I think the company will improve the offer. From my experience, I can assure you that if you don't ask, generally you will not receive. There are a few exceptions to this rule, and they generally involve difficult to fill positions or senior executive positions. If there is an item you would like to receive in an offer that is not included, keep in mind that if you do not receive it up front, the probability of getting it relatively soon is minimal. Don't be hesitant to suggest an improvement be made to an offer. Some employers take the position that when they make an offer, that's it, and they will make no changes. Others make an offer at a lower salary or compensation level recognizing they may need to raise the offer. In a lean job market with plentiful surplus talent, employers tend to be less flexible than in a tight employment market where employers have to compete for talent.

Remember, assuming you can't negotiate an offer can be costly. I have seen many situations where candidates could have obtained better offers but did not, simply for lack of asking or not being persistent. I have seen changes made by some companies considered hard-line rigid "no negotiations" types and little yielding by others who were considered more flexible. I have seen offers changed in all types of market conditions, by all types of companies—conservative, liberal, you name it—when good reasons accompany the changes requested or market conditions require it. The following suggestions are broad-based guidelines used to improve an offer:

- Obtain data on comparable rates for the position from applicable sources, such as compensation surveys, other companies in the same industry, individuals in the same or similar positions, search companies, your present job (if applicable), and other jobs and job offers you have had.
- If you feel the offer is low or inadequate, inquire about the basis on which the offer was made.
- Determine if the company is aware of competitive rates and compensation study results. Share your job search results and data gathered regarding compensation. Suggest a meeting to review the offer, at which time you can utilize data obtained to illustrate your suggestion regarding the offer.
- In your discussion, talk about your better performance level in comparison to others and the norm. Mention your years of experience and future contributions to the company. Stress your advantages and how they add value to the company.
- Stay focused on the items of key importance to the job and company. Be positive and avoid any form of criticism. You can avoid criticism by never offering your personal opinion. Make sure the impression you give is that of thoughtful consideration. Do not come across as demanding.
- I do not recommend sending the company a letter to attempt to negotiate a change, particularly a compensation improvement. If unable to meet personally, use the telephone. Only send a letter for follow-up purposes. Often several parties can be involved in a possible offer change, and a letter may be misunderstood.
- Encourage the employer to revise the offer in a range you have discussed. Always indicate you have given the offer careful consideration before suggesting the changes desired. If there is more than one item involved, attempt to settle the most workable issues first to establish a positive environment for the most difficult items to negotiate.

- Termination agreements and employment contracts in some employment relationships are important considerations. They can be an advantage for both the job hunter and employer. In certain situations they are essential—at high levels and in high-risk environments.

Termination Agreements and Employment Contracts

I am frequently asked by candidates how often such agreements are offered, particularly by the company they are considering. Depending upon the level and importance of the position involved in the company, both come into play in varying degrees.

Generally, employment contracts are used for executive and certain senior-level management positions. They are infrequently used at lower levels unless need dictates. Termination agreements are a more recent adjunct to employment agreements and are used on a limited basis.

As to the question by job hunters on how realistic it is to expect to receive an employment contract or termination agreement, the answer most often lies in the following. The job hunter generally needs to initiate discussion and request an agreement to support the need. Ask yourself the following questions to determine whether there is a need:

1. Do you need it? (Is there an employment risk involved? Relocation? Substantial potential loss of employment? Special risk conditions?)
2. Is it an appropriate level position for such an agreement?
3. Are there market, business, or proprietary requirements (for example, noncompetitive or confidentiality needs) for such an agreement?
4. Do job market conditions create a need?
5. Is there a need for a comprehensive agreement (length, time, responsibilities, and specific objective to accomplish)?

Termination and contract agreements are further extensions of the typical offer agreement letter. The termination agreement is generally less complex and detailed than an employment contract. It establishes a specific period during which the employer agrees to pay the employee regardless of continued employment (in other words, if the employee is let go or loses the job through no fault of his or her own during that period of time, compensation will be made to cover that period of time.)

Contract agreements are more comprehensive and detailed. They often cover items involving length of time, job responsibilities and duties, the way the company may terminate the agreement or working relationship, total compensation, and other matters. The use of such agreements has increased over the years.

The growing importance of such agreements as a natural expansion of the common offer-letter agreement is emphasized by the business uncertainties that exist in today's dramatically changing business world and job market as described in Chapters 1 and 2.

Accepting or Rejecting Your Job Offer

You have an offer! If the offer is sufficiently acceptable to be given serious consideration, do the following:

- Take plenty of time to consider the offer before accepting, rejecting, or renegotiating it.
- Consider the offer in light of your goals and objectives. Evaluate the offer in terms of how it compares to either your prior job (if unemployed) or your present job and your needs and expectations.
- Ask yourself if there are other job offers or potential offers you want to consider.
- Ask yourself if you have sufficient data about the company, its organization, its people, and the market it serves. What is the future for the company and you?
- If employed, does the new job offer you significant advantages over your current one? Does it provide something you do not currently receive in your current job that is significant enough to make the change worthwhile? Make sure you are not changing jobs just for the sake of change or to solve a temporary issue.
- If you are seriously interested, weigh the pros and cons of the offer. Keep in mind that accepting a new job is a serious move and can have a significant impact on your career. If the job does not work out, you will need to repeat the process, and, most importantly, learn what went wrong. There is also the possibility of becoming locked into a poor job longer than you would like.

Many senior job hunters who have been through the job change process more than once indicate a solid double check (yes or no review) system has worked best for them in making a final job offer decision. This involves setting aside your decision for several days to a week without thinking about it. Return to the decision after that time and see if it is still the same. If so, you will find you have probably reached a sound conclusion. Should you change your mind, review your decision-making process again.

If you need more information at that point to help your decision process, get it. It is not unusual to see candidates change their minds, sometimes several times, before reaching a final conclusion. This is why it is important to persuade the employer to allow you enough time to make the right decision for you. The amount of time to make a decision can vary, depending on many factors. Some individuals feel comfortable in making a decision within several days; for others, it may be several weeks. I normally urge at least one to two weeks to allow time to gather all input for the decision and then reflect on it for a period of time. If you are pushed on time by the employer, point out to them that it is vitally important to you and to the company that the decision is properly thought out. It is worthwhile to point out that you don't want to accept today if you are not 100 percent sure—and then in two to three weeks advise the company you have changed your mind, after the employer has turned away all other possible candidates.

If you decide to accept an offer, request a copy of the offer in writing. Sign and return a copy of the letter acknowledging your acceptance. If no written offer letter is provided, then confirm in writing your understanding of the offer, including all major terms and conditions.

Rejection and Other Opportunities

Should you decide to reject an offer, do so in a positive manner by telephone or in a personal meeting. If you have had difficulty in making a rejection decision, indicate this to the company. Offer rejections are common for many reasons. Reply in a timely fashion, and make sure the company understands your reasons for rejection. Follow up your discussions with a personal letter thanking them for their time and interest. Your rejection discussion is a good time for you to build additional rapport for the purpose of future opportunities with the company or referrals from the company.

If you are interested in other positions within the company, make sure the proper person knows and keep in touch with this person on a regular basis. A word of caution! In today's lean job market, I do not recommend using a rejection as a negotiating tool to get a better offer. The chances are it won't work and is not worth the risk. If you want to change certain aspects of an offer, work on negotiating the offer before rejecting it.

Your decision can be one of the more important ones you will make during your career and perhaps during your lifetime. Take your time, study every angle, and if you are reluctant, ask yourself why. In the Workbook available, you will find a detailed listing of the employment-offer items listed by category along with additional offer-analysis questions.

After you decide to accept an offer, take time to celebrate! You have worked hard, and you deserve some fun before you settle in with your new company for more hard work.

Your New Job

A new job leads to new opportunities and challenges. To assure that you take advantage of your new job opportunity, utilize the 25 working suggestions available in the Workbook on "Getting Started in Your New Job on The Right Foot."

SURVEY SUGGESTIONS

From Hiring Managers

- Don't waste time mailing nondirected resumes.
- Be determined.
- Network. Network. Network.

From Job Hunters

- Don't use blanket resume efforts; they're a waste.
- Don't let on that you are desperate.
- Know about the employers you contact.

14

Strategies for Problems and Special Situations

It is clear that the economy has turned corporate America and the job market upside down. As corporate America restructures itself, those left out in the cold are faced not just with finding a new job, but in a surprising number of cases a whole new career. For millions of Americans, the days of beginning and ending a career with one company are coming to an end. Many wonder how to avoid job changes. In some cases, there simply is no way to avoid them.

If you think you've got problems, take comfort in the fact that there's always someone right around the corner with problems a lot worse than yours. We'll start with the simple problems and build up to the more complex ones. Let's suppose you've been searching for a job for the past eight months. You've sent out 500 resumes, been called in for three interviews, and received no job offers. What a downer! What next?

Start by reviewing your job search from start to finish. Make sure your objectives are realistic and are solidly based on your background, experience, skills, and special talents. Review the following checklist to see where you may need to improve:

- Attitude
- Performance
- Networking techniques

- Presentation techniques
    Introductory calls
    Resume
    Cover letter
    Interview
- Skills applicable to job market need
- Experience suitable for current employer need
- Job search methods and techniques

Evaluate your job market approach, your sources, and your target lists. Evaluate your skills and experience. Recognize that:

1. You must possess skills that are marketable and in demand for today's job market.
2. You are responsible for developing and maintaining those skills; today those skills should be crossfunctional. (See Chapter 6.)
3. The demand (business/industry movement) for increased skills is axiomatic; it now requires continuous training to meet the needs of the new lean operating business era. (See Chapters 1 and 2.)

Develop a positive profile of yourself (skills, experience, training, education, special talents. (See Chapter 6.) Accentuate those positives every day, and soon they will become a permanent part of you.

If you are really struggling, look into obtaining job counseling services. The major outplacement companies may be able to recommend an appropriate person to you as well. In addition, the better firms can refer psychologists utilized for outplacement work. You can also contact Job Hunter Help Groups through appropriate professional organizations, such as Forty Plus and others. Working out your problems with a group can lead to new insights. You will also find it helpful to work the lengthy personal assessment checklist available in the workbook.

You may need to consider alternatives, such as recareering, additional training, consulting assignments, part-time or temporary work, volunteer work, relocation, self-employment, and entrepreneuring. Some of these areas will also provide additional networking opportunities and job leads. The important thing to remember is that no matter what your problem, there is usually a solution. The following story is one individual's solution to overcoming extreme adversities.

Lawrence Anderson thought he had his future all mapped out. He played catcher for the varsity baseball team while attending the University of San Francisco. He had plans to become a professional baseball player, and things were beginning to fall into place. Yet in just a few seconds, his dreams were shattered. He was in an automobile accident and became paralyzed.

At first he was overwhelmed by the difference between the tremendous amount of energy one possesses at 21 versus the incredible restrictions his injury had created. Slowly, he broke through many of these restrictions in his determination to lead a productive life.

Lawrence graduated from The University of San Francisco and then attended Arizona State Law School. His long-term ambition is to be a Federal District Court Judge. Now as a Superior Court Judge, he is greatly admired by his peers.

The road since the accident has certainly not been a smooth one. Recently, an organization that charters thousands of youth athletic teams attempted to prevent Lawrence from coaching a local athletic team, citing his wheelchair as a threat to player safety. Lawrence, whose son was on his team, said that if he thought there were any danger to the players, he would not be on the field. Parents and players from both his team and opposing teams, wholeheartedly supported Lawrence's position on the matter. The issue was resolved in a court decision based on the Americans with Disabilities Act. The court decided in his favor. Lawrence was allowed to continue coaching.

It is clear that Lawrence knows how to overcome obstacles. In addition to his role as Superior Court Judge and coach, he manages to both ski and scuba dive when he can get away from the courthouse.

If Lawrence can persevere under such severe restrictions, surely you can dig in your heels and find a successful solution to your own problems.

Type of Problems Most Often Encountered

The following are the types of problems most job hunters report in their job search:

- Lack of response/no jobs available
- Rejection
- Lack of skills
- Over age 50
- Time gaps

- Reentering the job market
- Discrimination
- Disabilities

When Problems Occur— Complete a Job Search Checkup

When problems do occur, complete a personal and job market check-up to make sure you have a real problem rather than just a temporary frustration, delay, or lull in your job search efforts. Be patient. If a problem does exist, take a good look at yourself as you evaluate and analyze your options. Ask yourself if it is the job market that is the problem or a lack of talent, training, education, or verbal/written/ presentation skills on your part.

Survival Questions to Ask Yourself

In any case, ask yourself the following questions to see if they apply:

- Am I up-to-date on the job market?
- Am I matching my skills and experience to employer needs (PEG matching)?
- Am I meeting the needs of what the job market requires?
- Do I have an action plan, and am I executing it?
- Am I nontraditional as well as traditional in my job search techniques and sources (TNT)?
- Am I seeking professional guidance in my job search?
- Am I willing to relocate or recareer?
- Am I applying the TART guide (turn around/retry/retrain)?

After you have answered these questions, review the other lessons of earlier chapters. Now, take another look at yourself. Make sure your objectives are realistic and are solidly based on your background, experience, and skills.

Grade Yourself on the Following Skills:

Presentation

- Your personal presentation, dress, style, and grooming.
- Your attitude and demeanor. Are you positive and confident? Overbearing and too assertive? Too passive?

Verbal and Nonverbal Skills

- Your introduction, telephone presentation, interview skills, and voice projection.
- Your tone of voice, body language, and facial expression.

Job Skills

- Are they up-to-date, adequate, or inadequate for today's job market?
- Do skills need to be upgraded or new ones developed to compete in the job market?
- If recareering, are your skills transferable?

Education/Experience

- Is your education and experience level adequate to compete for the jobs for which you are applying?
- Are additional training and education, new training and education, or a new degree and credentials needed?

Other Elements in Your Checkup

If you have been searching for a job for a lengthy period of time you should reassess your job search plan and strategy as well as the job search process you are using to attain your goals. If there are no jobs available for your skills, you will want to check with outplacement specialists, career counselors, placement industry specialists, industry sources, and Department of Labor forecasts to see whether the shortage is temporary or long term and whether your skills have become obsolete. If either of the latter situations is the case, you should develop new skills applicable to current market demands or transfer your skills to a more in-demand job area. Oftentimes one missing piece in a job search plan and presentation can make the difference between the ideal job and a marginal job or no job.

Go back and rework the assessment process in Chapter 6 and the matching process in Chapter 9. Also reassess your presentation (VWP). (See Chapters 9 and 10.) When you know you've got a competitive job search plan and presentation with skills to match today's employer job needs, then do what you must utilizing the five new guides, etc. to create an aura of success around yourself. That will give the employer the confidence to hire you. Make sure that any stress and frustration you may feel do not become outwardly apparent. If you feel continually frustrated, take a break for a few days to a week and rethink your approach. Remember, the *Hiring Manager Survey* pointed out that communication and presentation are the number one and two shortcomings of job hunters. The *Employer Survey* pointed out the number one shortcoming was unrealistic expectations and number two and three were communication and presentation. Ask yourself if the above shortcomings apply to you. These problems can be corrected with fresh insight, patience, and the knowledge that many job hunters deal with them and move on to a more effective and successful job search effort.

Take Positive Action

Once you've reorganized your job search plan or presentation, enlist the help of all of the sources we have covered to get a fresh supply of leads.

Don't accept a lack of response from your various contacts and the ads you have answered. After two weeks, redraft your inquiry using a different introduction and approach. Match your strengths to company needs and embellish your message with accomplishments and the contributions you can make to the company. In your company contacts where opportunities are discovered or available, call and get the name of the hiring manager. Speak with that person or a designated assistant. Ask about the essential qualifications and describe your advantages; follow up promptly.

Take positive action in those areas you have pinpointed for changing, improving, or updating. Draw up a plan for every day of the week, including Saturday, and stick to it! Don't let fear of the unknown stop you from investigating nontraditional approaches and the behind-the-scenes and hidden job markets. In an *employer's job market,* these avenues often provide the most fertile opportunities.

Forgotten Talents

If you have not completed a careful self-analysis of your skills and experience as suggested in Chapter 6, you may have a gold mine of potential you have forgotten about. To discover this potential, review Chapter 6 and the following areas:

- Early experiences
- Special training
- Skills not recently used
- Craft/hobby activities that could become moneymakers
- Community, fundraising, and similar activities

These areas can open up new opportunities. You might choose to become an entrepreneur, self-employed, or part of a joint venture with others. You could become a consultant or part of a franchising operation. Network marketing is a possibility. Or you might choose to work out of your home in a service business like data management, market research and analysis, catering, home repairs, electronic/technical service, or a shopping service. The opportunities are endless. It just takes creativity, innovation, and in some cases the willingness to take some risks.

Let's take a look at a couple of success stories.

Success Stories

Lloyd was cutback from his job as general manager of an electronics company at the age of 57. Struggling to find an appropriate full-time general manager position, he began seeking consulting work based on his strengths in industrial operations and production engineering. He landed a consulting assignment in industrial engineering and completed it successfully. It was then extended. After several months, the company recognized that Lloyd had just the kind of talent and experience they were looking for and made him an offer to be general manager, which he happily accepted.

Jerry was laid off from a *Fortune* 500 company dealing in aircraft, aerospace, and industrial products. Jerry was the vice president of operations and had an excellent background in operations, manufacturing, and engineering, with a proven record of performance. After many months of no luck in finding a new job, Jerry began looking for a business to purchase that would utilize his skills and experience. After thorough research, he acquired a sign company with his own funds. The company is now expanding into new markets, and Jerry is thrilled with its success. He responded to a tight job market by creating his own opportunity. So can you.

Ted was laid off from a major electronics and aerospace company. After looking for a full-time corporate opportunity for months without success, he became a successful consultant. As such, he bettered his previous salary level of the past two years. Ted is now seeking to return to the industry, but in the meantime will continue his consulting business. He is another example of someone who seized the initiative and made a job opportunity happen.

These people took positive action in a negative situation by utilizing their capabilities and forging ahead in nontraditional areas. All set a goal, were willing to work hard, and took some risk to reach their goal. These success stories attest to the value of being determined, moving forward in a positive manner, and keeping your spirits up!

Many of the individuals I talk with have followed the basic steps in their job search—up to a certain point. At that point, productive work comes to a halt, and most often these individuals end up relying on traditional job search techniques. By doing so, they tap only into visible job opportunities, which today could be less than 40 percent of the jobs available. When these same individuals are turned on to developing job opportunities via more aggressive nontraditional job hunting techniques, they often achieve surprising results.

Working nontraditional techniques requires breaking the mold of what worked in past years and moving on to more effective techniques. Initially it requires becoming more assertive and thorough in working all facets of the job market.

Handling Rejection

When you contact people outside your normal group, some may not personally warm up to you as an individual, or they may not find your qualifications suitable. Rejection, therefore, is to be expected. Don't be turned off by it.

Learn from rejection. Be quick to land on your feet and respond positively to negative comments. Endeavor to turn rejection around by understanding the points of rejection, answering questions, and then pointing out the favorable benefits that can be derived from what the interviewer perceives as negative. In your job search, you may be rejected for many reasons—some valid, some not valid, and some questionable.

The best way to handle negatives and rejection is to be well prepared for your interview. Don't accept a no or a rejection letter if you feel confident you are qualified. Call or write the hiring manager and rework the process. Review your qualifications with them. They may have passed over important information. If nothing else, you can develop a friendly relationship with the hiring or human resources manager, who may give you further leads.

If you are continually rejected over a long period of time, you must review your strategy, presentation, and qualifications. It may be time to seek professional advice or retrain/recareer. If there is a common recurring factor in the no's you receive, either in your skills and experience or inventory of capabilities, you need to be aware that these areas being assessed by the employer may be weak. Also, your presentation may need improvement. Whatever the reason, take immediate action. The sooner you do, the sooner you'll be working again.

Retraining

Some companies are retraining employees in their restructuring and downsizing process. This is an excellent opportunity to learn new skills while you are being paid. It will also allow you to stay at your present company and keep your benefits.

If you hear rumors that your company is going to restructure or downsize, you may want to (either on your own, or as part of a group) suggest the company consider retraining to improve effectiveness and as an alternative for some downsizing.

If you find your own skills need to be upgraded, don't delay in getting started in your training activity. Whether employed or not, your skills are the basic asset you have to offer an employer and any delay in improvement can be costly. Seek out whatever training is available. Don't wait for someone to come along and provide it for you. In learning about job market needs, the jobs in demand, and the emerging industries, don't hesitate to gather data from the U.S. Department of Labor on their job growth projections and training program activity. Also, talk to human resources managers, particularly those in leading and emerging industries, to learn what companies are seeking and what jobs and careers are more in demand. The *Employer Survey* results (Chapter 3) provide useful information on both skills in demand and jobs that are difficult to fill.

Make it happen. You will be surprised at the value these upgraded skills provide in your job search repertoire.

Federal and State Training Programs

If you must retrain in order to recareer, there are many schools and training centers to serve your needs. If you're not sure what's available to you, check with your local Chamber of Commerce, the yellow pages, your city council member, the State Department of Employment, and the U.S. Department of Labor. Early in 1994, the U.S. Department of Labor sketched out plans for a nationwide reemployment network that would offer unemployment compensation, career counseling, job training, and placement. This initiative would combine federal, state, and local job training, as well as placement programs, into a single system to provide uniform services and information to jobless workers nationwide. The proposal, contained in the Workforce Security Act, is one piece of broad Administration policy that would change the government's relationship with American livelihoods and the nation's workplaces. It would serve people in a wide range of economic groups—from laid-off high-tech workers to unskilled workers.

"We are creating a system that links people to jobs and to the information and resources they need to get their next job," Labor Secretary Robert Reich said in a recent interview. Reich explained that the reemployment program would be phased in. If it is successful, he said, "within five or six years America will have a one-stop shopping employment system."[1]

Recareering

Many job hunters are recareering to another job area or profession. For some it is a blessing in disguise. Think of all the people you've talked with who have mentioned how bored they are with their job and how, one of these days, they're going to get out of their rut and do something fulfilling . . . something they "want" to do. This is the moment they've been waiting for! If you are thinking about recareering, it will be helpful for you to review Chapter 6.

Many of your skills are transferable. Let's review some of the more valuable transferable skills and attributes:

- Managing
- Public speaking
- Problem solving
- Organizing
- Leadership
- Selling
- Decision making
- Negotiating

- Analysis, evaluation
- Planning
- Creativity
- Teaching
- Information processing
- Presentation
- Writing

---

1. "Job Market Expansion is Reich's Top Priority," *Los Angeles Times,* 11 October 1993.

The following examples illustrate how someone whose job became obsolete was successful in recareering.

Joan was an art director for a major retailer. She was let go when the computer system was upgraded to perform the necessary graphics functions and all art work was relegated to the computer. Joan had always had a talent for interior decorating and redirected her career to that area. She is now a full-time interior decorator and is often called upon to decorate the home furnishing's department of her former employer.

Jeff was a pilot of commercial seaplanes until the FAA decided they were too old to be safe. The aircraft went to a museum. Jeff decided to get together with several fellow pilots and form a charter airline for commuters. The company is thriving, and Jeff is making three times the money he made as a seaplane pilot.

If you are considering recareering, remember the areas of candidate shortcomings and skills need cited by the *Hiring Manager* and *Employer Surveys*:

- Personal computer skills
- Industry-specific training
- Hands-on experience
- Participative management style
- Transferable skills
- Cross-functional skills
- Innovative risk taking
- Team player
- Communication
- Presentation skills
- Leadership skills
- Strategic planning
- Visionary thinking

Jobs in demand are in the research/scientific area, as well as in engineering design, software, medical (RN and physical therapy), environmental, marketing/sales, and customer support services. Jobs drastically cut in the corporate restructuring process include administrative and middle management, as well as many executive positions.

The key to your success in recareering is double-sided. First, you must transform your skills to job market segments where they are in demand. Second, you must use the *99 Minute Formula,* VWP Guide, and PEG matching techniques learned in preceding chapters.

Remember in your recareering and retraining to look at jobs in emerging fields that provide growth opportunities. Examples include telecommunications, multimedia, biotechnology, health care, medical support services, satellite communications, electronics, financial services, infrastructure (local, county, state, and federal), desktop publishing, technical writing/publication, and computer networking. Try to match your skills and interest to the growing areas of job market needs and wants, particularly those of emerging businesses.

Over 50

If you are over 50, write your resume in a manner that makes your age difficult, hopefully impossible, to determine. Leave out the date of your degree, briefly summarize your early experience, and cut off your years of experience at twenty-five.

Keep in mind that temporary employment can lead to permanent employment. Consulting assignments can lead to full-time employment. Once an employer learns of your competence, age bias often disappears. In recent years, I have seen this happen often.

Many over-50 job hunters are using their experience to venture into all forms of business, starting a company, buying a business, becoming a distributor, or turning an invention into a business. The possibilities are endless. I can also cite many examples where individuals over 60 were successful in starting a business and going on to a new world of challenge they never thought possible.

One such story involves Nick, who is 67 years old and very busy in a business venture he started completely on his own. He purchased the patent of a newly designed product applicable to the consumer and industrial products market. After improving on the product and developing a successful nationwide market, he found a suitable manufacturer and is now marketing the product nationwide through various distribution and direct sales outlets. Recently, several companies expressed interest in purchasing the product. Nick indicates he may sell his interest and continue to gain a percentage of every product item sold.

Forty Plus

Forty Plus is a self-help organization for unemployed executives. There are over 15 independently operated offices in various cities throughout the country. Members of this nonprofit organization receive substantial career guidance, peer support, interviewing, and networking assistance. Forty Plus actively works to receive job listings and assists its participants in their job search efforts.

Time Gaps

Be prepared to answer questions regarding any time gaps in your resume. While a time gap due to a job loss (downsizing, reorganization, plant closure), no longer carries the stigma it once did, a job hunter needs to answer any questions in a straightforward manner. After responding, if you are further pressed, respond again affirmatively and move the interview on to positive areas, stressing your assets and strengths. Do not muddle your way through such questions. Hesitancy in handling questions of this nature often causes concern. Being well prepared helps in handling most interview questions.

There are many good reasons for time gaps such as:

- Family/business
- Early retirement
- Special training
- Armed Services

- Illness
- Bad timing/layoff
- Education
- Volunteer work

Reentering the Job Market

Loss of skills or lack of skills for the current job market are perceived by employers as the biggest problem faced by job hunters reentering the job market. Before you reenter the market, compare your skills and experience (Chapter 6) to job market need (PEG matching, Chapter 9) to determine what possible training, new skills, or recareering efforts you must make.

One item of concern to some employers is the length of time and cause of the applicant being out of the job market. The question often asked is, "Why were you out of the job market, and what have you done to keep your yourself up-to-date?" Planning and preparing to reenter the job market will immensely improve the process and shorten the time involved.

It is important to know what is going on in the job market so you can properly target companies that are compatible with your experience. In addition, you will need to place special emphasis on marketing and selling yourself (Chapters 9 through 13). When an employer questions your length of time out of the job market, you must be able to make an excellent presentation of your skills, experience, and the contributions you can make to the company (VWP) to convince the employer that not only are you qualified, but you are the person for the job.

Illegal Questions

The Equal Opportunity Commission (EEOC) issued the "Uniform Guidelines on Employer Selection Procedures" in 1978. The following is a list of the major laws dealing with Equal Opportunity:

- Civil Rights Act of 1991
- Age Discrimination in Employment Act of 1967, amended 1978, 1986
- Rehabilitation Act of 1973
- Pregnancy Discrimination Act—1978
- Immigration Reform and Control Act (IRCA)—1986

Questions that relate to hiring decisions regarding age, race, color, religion, sex, national origins, disabilities, and certain other areas are illegal. Additionally, certain questions about spouses, pregnancy, organization memberships, child care arrangements, and arrest are generally prohibited or limited. Job hunters should also be aware that sending a photograph of themselves to employers when submitting a resume or during the screening process, is not recommended.

The Job Hunter Survey shows that illegal questions are still being asked and must be dealt with in a positive manner to avoid turning off the interviewer. Various approaches can be used in responding to such questions. For example, if asked about your age, be positive. Answer, "I am a hard worker, willing to work long hours, have lots of energy, many times greater, in fact, than people much younger. Most of all, I am a wiser and smarter worker because of my years of experience." If you are pressed, ask the interviewer to repeat the question and again respond in a positive manner. If continually pressed, be straightforward in expressing your concern that your answer to the question may provide information that would place the employer in the position of seeking information that is discriminating and illegal.

Help for Those with Disabilities

The Americans With Disabilities Act states that employers must provide reasonable accommodation for people with disabilities; that is, they must provide change in the work environment or in the way things are usually done that results in an equal employment opportunity for an individual with a disability.

An employer must make a reasonable accommodation to the known physical or mental limitations of a qualified applicant or employee with a disability, unless it can be shown that such accommodation would cause an undue hardship on the operation of the business. Some examples of reasonable accommodation include:

- Job restructuring
- Modifying work schedules
- Reassignment to a vacant position; acquiring or modifying equipment or devices
- Adjusting or modifying examinations, training materials, or policies

An organization called Disability 2000 is made up of the CEOs of 2000 major U.S. corporations. The council's goal is to double the employment of people with disabilities in America's workforce by the year 2000. Contact with Disability 2000 can be made at 202/293-5960 through Martin Walsh. An additional group that may be helpful to you if you have a disability and are looking for employment are the Job Accommodation Network in Morgantown, West Virginia (800/526-7234).

People with disabilities can have outstanding careers with impressive accomplishments. We mentioned Judge Lawrence Anderson in the beginning of the chapter. Another success story is Andrea Friedman. Andrea was born with Down's Syndrome. Her pediatrician stated that her condition was hopeless and suggested her parents institutionalize her. They disagreed with the doctor and brought her up their own way. Today, Andrea is a successful actress. She played the role of Corky's girlfriend/wife in the ABC hit series *Life Goes On.* Recently, Andrea made a guest appearance on *Baywatch,* and she is up for a starring role in a new movie. When she isn't acting, she goes to college. How does she get there? She drives! In fact, Andrea is one of the few people in the world with Down's Syndrome who drives a car—and in the busy city of Los Angeles, no less. If Andrea can have a successful career with hard work and determination, so can you!

Receiving the Offer Can Be Difficult

Sometimes an employer can agonize over developing and presenting an offer to a job hunter. The employer may not be able to decide between two or three people or may be only 90 percent sure, or the hiring person may be a person who doesn't like to make commitments. In these instances, you must ask for the offer by stating something like: "I really feel that I'm ideally suited for this job, do you?" If the employer continues to hesitate, stay put in your chair as if you intend to stay until you get the offer. Keep telling the employer how much you want the job, like the company, and so on. A woman I know utilized this plan successfully. So can you. Of course, there are many other ways to entice a reticent employer. Act on what's comfortable and what works for you.

Few problems are insurmountable. If you are qualified for a position, there is no reason why you can't overcome obstacles as long as you act in a tactful and positive manner.

The competition is tough, but if you've got the qualifications and experience and know how to present and sell yourself, you can put yourself on track to win the ideal job.

SURVEY SUGGESTIONS

From Hiring Managers

- Never stop looking for work—it's there somewhere.
- Take temporary assignments.
- Persevere.

From Job Hunters

- Join Forty Plus.
- Prepare several resumes highlighting different strengths.
- Keep a positive attitude, network, and never give up.

Appendix A
Questions Often Asked of Candidates

Employer/Former Employer Questions

1. Why are you changing jobs? Why did you leave your last employer or former employers?
2. What happened on your last job? Were you laid off, terminated, or did you voluntarily quit?
3. Why were you laid off, terminated, or fired?
4. How do you feel about your employer or former employer? How do you feel about being laid off or terminated?
5. What salary/compensation were you earning?
6. What do you like most and least about your job? Your prior jobs?

Job Performance Questions

1. What kind of performance reviews did you receive? How often and how were you rated by your boss?
2. How is/was your job performance measured? How do you measure the job performance of your subordinates?
3. In what areas did your supervisor rate you high and low?
4. What were considered to be your major strengths and weaknesses by your superiors? Do you agree with their conclusions?
5. What have you accomplished in your present job? In your prior positions and jobs?

Questions about Relating with Others

1. How well did you get along with your supervisor, his boss, your peers and subordinates?
2. How well do you think your supervisor got along with you?
3. What were your relationships with others in your department, and the company? With whom did you work most closely?
4. What other individuals, peers, and subordinates did you closely work with or relate to? How did those relationships develop and what were the results?
5. Who did you work most effectively with, least effectively with, and why?

Personal Preference Questions

1. What can you tell me about yourself? Describe yourself and your personality.
2. Why should I hire you? Why should our company hire you?
3. What are your career goals, work goals, and personal goals and objectives?
4. What commendations did you receive and what suggestions for improvements were made?
5. What are your major strengths and weaknesses?
6. What are you looking for in a new job? Why are you interested in this job, and what are your expectations?

Sink or Swim Questions

1. What kind of contribution do you feel you could make to our company and how long would it take?
2. What is there about our company that interests you?
3. How would you sell our product and company?
4. Describe your career, its progression, and what you have accomplished. What are your future plans?
5. What salary/compensation are you looking for?

Schooling, Formal Education and Training Questions

1. What is the extent of your formal education? What degrees and diplomas have you earned?
2. What additional training and schooling have you had?

3. Have you had any special training (management, professional, technical, trade, craft, etc.)?
4. Why did you decide on (specific area/s, i.e. environmental sciences)?
5. What was your major and why?
6. What activities and school leadership responsibilities were you involved in?

Appendix B
Job Source Information

L iterally hundreds upon hundreds of valuable job sources are available. Depending upon your specific job, profession, and career interest pick those sources applicable to your needs from the directories, placement Industry sources, databases and databanks, job market listings/newsletters, business magazine/newspaper/indexes, and so on. Breakdown your job source information into categories. Most categories should provide valuable job source information. Keep in mind that one of the best sources of job infomation is your local public library or the University or College library nearest to you. The librarian can be most helpful. Some libraries have a business and directory section available, and some have database capabilities. The following highlights some of the basic sources of data available. A more detailed list is provided in the Workbook available separately. (See last page for information on the Workbook).

Source Directories
Chamber of Commerce directories, by city
Business directory guides by city, county, state, product/market
Business organization/Agencies Directory (Gale Research Inc.)
Directory/Corporation Affiliations (National Register Publishing Co.)
Directory of Management Consultants (Kennedy Publications)
Reference Book of Corporate Management (Dunn and Bradstreet)
Million Dollar Directory series (Dun's Marketing Services)

National Trade and Professional Associations (Colombia Books)
Manufacturers Directories (Manufacturers' News)
Standard & Poor's Register of Corporations, Directors, Executives
Thomas Register (Thomas Publishing Company)
Ward's Business Directory (Gale Research)
Directory of Human Resource Executives (Hunt- Scanlon Publishing)
Executive Employment Guide (American Management Association)
The Directory of Executive Recruiters (Kennedy Publications)
The Directory of Outplacement Firms (Kennedy Publications)

Computer Database and Banks

Dun's Marketing Service	Dialog
Moody's Rating	Dow Jones News Retrieval
Standard & Poors Register	Job Banks USA
Disclosure Online	Adnet Online
Lexis/Nexis	E-Span Inc.

General Job Market and Business Information Data

Exec-U-net Newsletter Job Listing
Search Bulletin & Netshare newsletter job listings
Job Market Directory (Career Communications)
National Business Employment Weekly (*Wall Street Journal*)
Associations with job help services (listings, data banks, etc.)
Ask Dow Jones/Journal Finder (*The Wall Street Journal*)
Article Clearinghouse
U.S. Industrial Outlook (U.S. Department of Commerce)
Where To Find Business Information (Brownstone and Curruth)
Various professional, association, and trade newspapers or journals
such as *Barrons, Business Week, Inc., Forbes, Fortune*

U.S. Department of Labor, Monthly and Quarterly Reports, etc.

1. U.S Government Printing Office, Washington, DC 20402
2. Bureau of Labor Statistics, 21 Massachusetts Ave, N.E., Room 2860, Washington, DC 20212, 202/606-5886 or 202/606-7828
3. U.S. Department of Commerce, National Information Service 5285 Port Royal Rd., Springfield, VA 22161

Index

How to Order the Job Search Workbook

To obtain a copy of the job search workbook call or fax the form below to:

(818) 568-0638

or you may send the form to:

Thomas Mangum Company
P.O. Box 50001
Pasadena, CA 91115-0001

Work materials include:

- Questions to ask yourself and the employer.
- A personal assessment check list.
- Comprehensive job search plan including working documents, resumes, letters, job description profile and samples, detailed sources with phone numbers, target company and offer items worksheet.
- A successful job search case study.
- Schedule/planner, master organizer overview worksheet, and contacts/call source work list.

Please send the job search workbook to:

Name (print) _____

Organization (if applicable) _____

Address _____

City _____ State _____ Zip _____

$12.95 plus handling and local sales tax.

_____ Check/Money order enclosed

_____ Master Card: #_____ Expiration _____

_____ Visa: #_____ Expiration _____

Signature _____

(for credit card)

handling/shipping ($2.90 for the 1st book, $.75 additional books)

Number of books _____   Price of books _____

All mail orders must be prepaid.   handling _____

Prefer immediate shipment (   ).

Allow for 4–6 weeks delivery where   tax _____

required by printing/backorders.   TOTAL _____

Information Update

We'd appreciate your input!

Additional job sources you believe are effective:

_____

_____

_____

_____

_____

Additional job search techniques you believe are effective:

_____

_____

_____

_____

Additional Comments:

_____

_____

_____

_____

Please send to: Thomas Mangum Company
                P.O. Box 50001,
                Pasadena, CA 91115-0001
                or fax to: 818/568-0638

Thank you